sächsische staatskapelle dresden

complete
discography
compiled by
john hunt

contents

7 introduction

31 discography

211 appendix a: false attributions

217 appendix b: index of conductors

241 appendix c: index of works

Sächsische Staatskapelle Dresden
Published by John Hunt.
Designed by Richard Chluparty
© 2002 John Hunt
reprinted 2009
ISBN 978-1-901395-10-5

Sole distributors:
Travis & Emery,
17 Cecil Court,
London, WC2N 4EZ,
United Kingdom.
(+44) 20 7 459 2129.
sales@travis-and-emery.com

some photographs courtesy of hansjoachim mirschel (including front cover of rudolf kempe with the orchestra) and erwin döring

acknowledgement

these publications have been made possible by contributions or advance subscription from the following

Stefano Angeloni	Stathis Arfanis	Yoshihiro Asada
Derek Bevan	E.C. Blake	Gordon Buffard
Edward Chibas*	Dennis Davis	F. De Vilder
John Derry	Hans-Peter Ebner*	Henry Fogel*
Nobuo Fukumoto	Peter Fülöp	Philip Goodman
Jean-Pierre Goossens	Johann Gratz	Michael Harris*
Tadashi Hasegawa*	Naoya Hirabayashi	Andrew Keener
Detlef Kissmann	John Larsen	Elisabeth Legge-Schwarzkopf*
Douglas MacIntosh	John Mallinson*	Carlo Marinelli
Philip Moores	Bruce Morrison	W. Moyle
Alessandro Nava	Alan Newcombe	Hugh Palmer*
Jim Parsons*	Laurence Pateman	David Patmore*
James Pearson	Tully Potter	Patrick Russell
Ingo Schwarz	Robin Scott	Tom Scragg*
Graham Silcock	Yoshihiko Suzuki*	Michael Tanner
Julian Tremayne	Urs Weber*	Graeme Wright*
Stephen Wright	Ken Wyman	Koji Kinoshita

*indicates life subscriber

Königliches  Opernhaus.

23. Vorstellung.
Montag, den 25. Januar 1909.

Richard Strauß=Woche.
1. Abend.
Uraufführung:

Elektra.

Tragödie in einem Aufzuge von Hugo von Hofmannsthal.
Musik von Richard Strauß.
Regie: Georg Toller.
Musikalische Leitung: Ernst von Schuch.

Personen:

Klytämnestra.	Ernestine Schumann-Heink.
Elektra,	Annie Krull.
Chrysothemis, } ihre Töchter.	Margarethe Siems.
Aegisth.	Johannes Sembach.
Orest.	Karl Perron.
Der Pfleger des Orest.	Julius Puttlitz.
Die Vertraute.	Gertrud Sachse.
Die Schleppträgerin.	Elisabeth Boehm-van Endert.
Ein junger Diener.	Fritz Soot.
Ein alter Diener.	Franz Nebuschka.
Die Aufseherin.	Riza Eibenschütz.
	Francista Bender-Schäfer.
	Magdalene Seebe.
Fünf Mägde.	Irma Tervani.
	Anna Zoder.
	Minnie Nast.

Dienerinnen und Diener. — Schauplatz der Handlung: Mykene.

Die Dekorationen sind vom Hoftheatermaler Rieck entworfen und angefertigt, die Kostüme nach Entwürfen des Professors Fanto vom Garderobe-Oberinspektor Metzger ausgeführt. Dekorative Einrichtung vom Oberinspektor Hasait.

Textbücher sind an der Kasse das Exemplar für 1 Mark zu haben.

Beurlaubt: Herr Rüdiger.

Der freie Eintritt ist ohne jede Ausnahme aufgehoben.
Gelöste Billetts werden nur bei Abänderung der Vorstellung zurückgenommen.

Spielplan.

Königliches Opernhaus.	Königliches Schauspielhaus.
Dienstag, 26. Januar. Richard Strauß-Woche. 2. Abend: Salome. Drama in einem Aufzuge. Musik von Strauß. Anfang 8 Uhr.	Dienstag, 26. Januar: Die Rabensteinerin. Schauspiel in vier Akten von E. v. Wildenbruch. Anfang ½8 Uhr.
Mittwoch, 27. Januar. Richard-Strauß-Woche. 3. Abend: Feuersnot. Singgedicht in einem Akt. Musik von R. Strauß. Symphonia domestica von Strauß. Anfang 8 Uhr.	Mittwoch, den 27. Januar: Die glücklichste Zeit. Lustspiel in drei Akten von Auernheimer. Anfang ½8 Uhr.

Einlaß 7 Uhr. Kasseneröffnung ½8 Uhr. Anfang 8 Uhr.
Ende ¾10 Uhr.

Sächsische Staatskapelle Dresden: introduction to the discography

Whilst preparing to document the recordings of the world's known second oldest symphony orchestra, I came across its description as *Wunderharfe* (magic harp), and wanted to check the origin of this highly flattering attribution. Does it come from some fawning critic or does it have a serious musicological source ? The compliment turns out to have been paid by none other than Richard Wagner, probably the central figure in a sequence of great composers from Heinrich Schütz through Antonio Vivaldi and Carl Maria von Weber to Richard Strauss, who had special associations with the *Sächsische Staatskapelle* over the years of its rich history. The orchestra returned the compliment in a most fitting manner when, in its 450 th jubilee concert in 1998 it programmed works which four of those composers (and the living composer Wolfgang Rihm) had written specifically for them.

For the first time in working on an orchestra discography I have enjoyed the collaboration of an orchestra member whose input has been invaluable in placing many details into perspective and in providing a mass of background information about the orchestra's recordings and its conductors both major and minor. Klaus Heinze will soon retire after four decades as a viola player (but his

fritz busch, generalmusikdirektor 1922-1933

son Wieland will continue in the first violin section) and is therefore specially qualified to report on the long years of work under totalitarian rule. What has impressed and helped me even more than his knowledge of the background to the recordings has been his serious dedication to the musical traditions stretching back into the first half of the twentieth century and further back still. This is a true combination of traditional values and German seriousness, for which I have come across no equivalent among British orchestral players whom I have met. Klaus is also typical of the orchestra as a whole in that he does not underplay the *Staatskapelle's* operatic connections as resident pit orchestra for the *Sächsische Staatsoper* in the manner which, for example, their counterparts in the *Wiener Philharmoniker* constantly do.

1924-1941
At the very outset of serious orchestral recording for the gramophone, which commenced at the end of the acoustic and the beginning of the electric eras, Dresden and its principal orchestra quickly became a centre for important activity. They may have lagged behind Berlin and Vienna in quantity of output, but certainly not in terms of musical quantity. It needs to be remembered that these were the musicians who, in the decades preceding their first recordings, had

karl böhm, generalmusikdirektor 1934-1942

premiered the Strauss operas *Salome, Elektra* and *Rosenkavalier* under the eminent conductor Ernst von Schuch.

As with much other orchestral output of the acoustic recording era, serious restoration employing modern digital techniques has yet to be applied to the 1924 Dresden sessions of Fritz Busch. Perhaps the Naxos label could investigate, as these recordings predate by a full ten years that conductor's work for HMV's Mozart Society edition from the Glyndebourne Festival. And the major series of Electrola sessions with Karl Böhm between 1936 and 1941 have so far received CD transfer only in Japan, although a fine set of LPs did emerge in Europe some twenty years ago. On the other hand, we do possess from these pre-war years several important documents of live performance (Busch – in sound and film – and Strauss with his beloved Dresden players on a 1936 visit to the Queens Hall London).

1941-1945
In retrospect we may come to thank, even if grudgingly, the various totalitarian régimes of the twentieth century for the importance which they placed on maintaining artistic values and on preserving much musical performance which would otherwise have receded into the memories of those present at the time. As the production of shellac discs became increasingly problematical under war-time conditions,

rudolf kempe, generalmusikdirektor 1950-1953

the newly-developed tape facilities of the *Reichsrundfunk* became as prolific in Dresden as in other musical centres: so that a wealth of the city's musical events – operas by Mozart, Goetz and Wolf, for example – were preserved under studio conditions for radio transmission.

1945-1954
This dissemination of radio broadcasts on tape continued after the cessation of hostilities, indeed was positively encouraged by record labels like Urania and Record Corporation of America, who were ready to pay the cash-strapped locals hard currency for the tapes which they put out in early LP pressings of often dubious quality (see also the appendix at the end of the discography, which details certain recordings bearing the name of Dresden State Orchestra which were actually not *Staatskapelle* productions). Now transferred to CD, we can enjoy productions of *Freischütz*, *Rosenkavalier* and *Die Meistersinger von Nürnberg* from that brief period when the Dresden-born Rudolf Kempe, the most dearly loved of all their musical directors, was in charge of opera and concerts before falling foul of the Communist administration and seeking his main career in the West.

kyrill kondrashin

From 1955
In the mid 1950s came the founding of the state-owned Eterna record label (VEB Deutsche Schallplatten), on which the *Staatskapelle* was to feature prominently for the next thirty-five years. The very first classical LP to be issued was Beethoven's *Eroica* played by the Dresden orchestra under Franz Konwitschny (this of course predates this conductor's better-known complete Beethoven cycle recorded with Dresden's immediate neighbours, the Leipzig Gewandhaus Orchestra). Music directors changed quite frequently during this early LP period, and most of them made some recordings with the orchestra which was now known simply as *Staatskapelle Dresden*, the Communist government not wishing to encourage any form of regional pride by referring to the Saxon connection. Guest conductors who also recorded with the *Staatskapelle* included the highly respected Russian Kyrill Kondrashin, who gave with them the first performances anywhere in Germany of Shostakovich's delayed, and only recently approved, Fourth Symphony (see session no. 099a). This is one of a considerable number of unpublished radio recordings and live performances included in the discography because of their significance – many more doubtless still languished undetected in the archives.

otmar suitner, generalmusikdirektor 1960-1964 but associated with the orchestra over a much longer period

Many Eterna LPs have been re-issued on the CD label Berlin Classics (see later note about other incarnations), most interesting among them being probably those with *Generalmusikdirektors* Otmar Suitner (1960-1964) and Herbert Blomstedt (from 1975 until virtually the end of Communist rule). Less prominent local conductors like Siegfried Kurz promoted contemporary East German composers for Eterna, although the chances of re-issue of such recordings seem more remote.

Starting in the 1960s and escalating in the 1970s, Eterna entered into co-productions with the Western recording companies EMI, Philips and Deutsche Grammophon. Many operas were featured under conductors like Karl Böhm, Herbert von Karajan and Carlos Kleiber, and also the orchestral works of Strauss under Rudolf Kempe and the Bruckner Symphonies under Eugen Jochum. These were valuable earners of foreign currency for the orchestra (and the German Democratic Republic!) and, equally important, maintained awareness in the West of Dresden's undiminished orchestral standards. However, today the orchestra does not feel that CD transfers of the material always do justice to the original LP editions. On one of my visits to Dresden I got proof of this when Klaus Heinze and I compared the opening of Bruckner's Seventh Symphony under Jochum on both the original LP and the CD re-issue: on the latter the orchestra's depth and warmth of

colin davis during a recording session

timbre, in every way equal to the best that the *Wiener Philharmoniker* can produce in this music, had obviously been compromised in a digital re-mastering.

Particular fondness is felt by orchestra members for British conductors who have worked with them - John Pritchard (no recordings) and more recently Colin Davis (at the time of writing they are eagerly anticipating a concert with Daniel Harding). But it is naturally the greatest figures from earlier years – Keilberth, Böhm, Kempe and Jochum – who are recalled with the deepest respect and affection. In the past decade a close rapport had been built up with Giuseppe Sinopoli, a partnership sadly ended this year by his sudden death. Here, I feel that it is the recordings taken down live by Deutsche Grammophon, rather than the sometimes studio-bound ones, that do the partnership most justice. And I always felt it most unfair that when the *Staatskapelle* visited Britain in recent years, the concert promoters did not summon the courage to have Sinopoli appear with them, presumably because of the inexplicable witch-hunt which certain British music critics instigated in the time when Sinopoli was chief conductor of the Philharmonia.

GIUSEPPE SINOPOLI (1946-2001) · LAST OPERA RECORDING
STRAUSS
Ariadne
auf Naxos
VOIGT · DESSAY
VON OTTER
HEPPNER · DOHMEN
STAATSKAPELLE DRESDEN
SINOPOLI

Recording venues
Surprisingly the bulk of the shellac discs cut with the orchestra by Böhm in the 1930s-1940s were made in the *Semperoper* itself, specially converted by Electrola's engineers (I use the house's common name, recalling the original architect Gottfried Semper, rather than the more correct *Sächsische Staatsoper*). After the building's total destruction in the 1945 bombings, concerts, operas and recordings had to take place in less than ideal substitute venues such as *Schauspielhaus* and *Hygienemuseum*. A new purpose-built *Kulturpalast* concert hall emerged in 1969, shared with Dresden's other orchestra, the *Dresdner Philharmonie*. Official recording venue during the LP era, after the converted *Kreuzkirche* was abandoned (early Deutsche Grammophon mono LPs were recorded here), was the *Lukaskirche*, which proved to be a perfect sound studio after its re-building. However, I was told a story of a Western prima donna who thought otherwise, causing the cancellation of one Philips opera project in the 1970s. The *Semperoper* itself, finally re-built and re-opened to great acclaim in 1984, was one of Communism's great cultural flagships, a truly splendid realisation, both acoustically and visually, of the original concept. It was only in 1992, however, and on Sinopoli's personal instigation, that the *Staatskapelle* decided to re-locate its own orchestral concerts there, after which it provided an ideal ambience for live and semi-live recordings.

NACHTRAG

zum Katalog 1959

VEB DEUTSCHE SCHALLPLATTEN

Eterna prefixes and categories
A highly practical numbering system of six digits was used, of which the main ones which concern us in this discography can be summarised. In the 1950s a smallish number of 45 rpm 7-inch discs (520 000) and 10-inch LPs (720 000) appeared, soon superseded by 12-inch LPs (820 000, 821 000 and 822 000) and with the advent of stereophonic recording new numberings (825 000, 826 000, 827 000, 725 000, 728 000 and 729 000 - the latter three during the 1980s when digitally-mastered LPs were introduced). Eterna's final prefix before its demise in 1989 was 329 000 for CDs. Separate LP categories had existed for lighter music (Amiga 845 000) and contemporary music (Nova 885 000). After the introduction of stereo, there appears to have been no consistent policy as to whether mono and stereo versions of a recording should always be issued, just as upon the introduction of CD some recordings continued to be published in an LP version and others not. Obviously the precarious finances of the German Democratic Republic in its final years meant that some joint productions with Western companies could no longer be issued in the East (Beethoven Piano Concerti with Christian Zacharias, Haydn Masses with Sir Neville Marriner, Evgeny Onegin with James Levine and Les Contes d'Hoffmann with Jeffrey Tate were some of these). East German CDs which did appear were again under the rubric *Deutsche Schallplatten*,

a term also used for Eterna LPs which had been published in Japan (these latter incarnations are not listed in the discography, in fact in common with other recent discographies I only list Japanese issues in cases where the material has not appeared elsewhere: as is well known by now the assiduous Japanese market for Western Classical music sees to it that virtually every Western label is available in Japan, albeit under its own independent numbering system). Since re-unification the contents of the Eterna catalogue has been distributed by a surprising number of short-lived offspring (Deutsche Schallplatten, Deutsche Schallplatten/Amabile, Ars vivendi, Berlin Classics and Corona Classics – the last two under the aegis of Edel Marketing). These labels have, in Britain at least, received only sporadic distribution: in Germany they can be found not only in record stores but also on market stalls and other outlets specialising in memorabilia from the old East Germany.

The recordings are grouped in sessions which often spread over a number of days or longer; however, this is not necessarily to suggest that recording took place on every intervening day. In many cases of co-productions with Western companies it transpired that recordings were completed ahead of the dates allocated. The sessions are numbered, and it is these numbers which are used for

OPERNHAUS

Donnerstag, am 14. Januar 1926, Anfang ½8 Uhr
11. Vorstellung für die Donnerstagreihe B

SALOME

Drama in einem Aufzuge nach Oscar Wildes gleichnamiger Dichtung
In deutscher Übersetzung von Hedwig Lachmann
Musik von Richard Strauß

Musikalische Leitung: Richard Strauß a. G.   Spielleitung: Georg Toller

Personen:

Herodes	Fritz Vogelstrom
Herodias	Irma Tervani
Salome	Eva Plaschke-v. d. Osten
Jochanaan	Robert Burg
Narraboth	Ludwig Eybisch
Ein Page der Herodias	Elfriede Haberkorn
Fünf Juden	Heinrich Teßmer / Ernst Meyerolbersleben / Richard Oswald / Hanns Lange / Ludwig Ermold
Zwei Nazarener	Willy Bader / Paul Schöffler
Zwei Soldaten	Julius Puttlitz / Robert Büssel
Ein Kappadozier	Heinrich Hermanns
Ein Page des Herodes	Erna Berger

Schauplatz: Eine große Terrasse im Palast des Herodes

Sämtliche Plätze müssen vor Beginn der Vorstellung eingenommen werden

Krank: Max Hirzel

Textbücher sind für 0,80 R.M. und Führer für 1,00 M.4 vormittags an der Kasse und abends bei den Türschließern zu haben

Gekaufte Karten werden nur bei Änderung der Vorstellung zurückgenommen

Einlaß u. Kassenöffnung ¾7 Uhr / Anfang ½8 Uhr / Ende geg. ¼10 Uhr

the various indices at the end of the discography, rather than page numbers. The published catalogue numbers of recordings in each main format (78rpm, 45rpm, LP, CD, VHS video, DVD video, DVD audio) are separated in the third column of the layout by a diagonal stroke/oblique.

Klaus Heinze has kindly placed at my disposal photographic and playbill material (including the cover photograph), some of which relates to performances on which a concurrent or subsequent recording was based. In addition to Klaus and Wieland Heinze I have to thank Richard Chlupaty, Ernst Lumpe and David Lampon for additional input, and Malcolm Walker for encouragemnent and help in identifying war-time Electrola recordings of operatic arias with the orchestra which remained unpublished in their 78rpm format probably due to shortage of raw materials, not to mention the bombing of the company's production plant in Berlin. However, I accept full personal responsibility for any errors or omissions, and am happy to hear from collectors who can help with additional data.

As already suggested, this orchestra's principal source of pride must be its participation in the world premieres of many a Richard Strauss opera under Schuch, Busch or Böhm. Some of that achievement is documented in the discography, with singers who actually took their

parts at a work's premiere (*Der Rosenkavalier, Daphne*). One of the first LP opera sets which I purchased as a young collector in the early 1960s was Karl Böhm's Dresden recording of *Elektra*. The significant connections between this orchestra and the work's composer may have been unknown to me at that time, but I was highly impressed by the integration of text and music and by the sovereign manner in which it was realised on those LPs. Certainly this is a case of first impressions being aroused whenever I am confronted with the work afresh, thanks in no short measure to the playing of the *Sächsische Staatskapelle Dresden*.

John Hunt 2001

001/may 1911/odeon sessions in berlin

strauss	unnamed conductor	odeon 80066
rosenkavalier	nast	cd: symposium 1227-1228
excerpt	van der osten	
(mir ist die		
ehre widerfahren)		

strauss	unnamed conductor	odeon 80067
rosenkavalier	nast	cd: symposium 1227-1228
excerpt	van der osten	
(mit ihren augen		
voll tränen)		

strauss	unnamed conductor	odeon 0-6412/80064/AA 79074
rosenkavalier	siems	cd: symposium 1227-1228
excerpt	nast	
(hab' mir's	van der osten	
gelobt)		

strauss	unnamed conductor	odeon 80065
rosenkavalier	nast	cd: symposium 1227-1228
excerpt	van der osten	
(ist ein traum)		

see note at bottom of page 32

002/25 august 1911/hmv sessions in berlin

strauss	unnamed conductor	hmv/grammophon 65200/
rosenkavalier	siems	HMB 55/043179
excerpt		lp: rococo R 20
(kann mich auch		cd: record collector TRC 10
an ein mädel)		cd: symposium 1227-1228
strauss	unnamed conductor	hmv/grammophon 65239/D 1002/
rosenkavalier	nast	043184
excerpt	van der osten	cd: symposium 1227-1228
(mit ihren augen		
voll tränen)		
strauss	unnamed conductor	hmv/grammophon 65200/044186
rosenkavalier	siems	lp: rococo R 20
excerpt	nast	lp: preiser CO 428
(hab' mir's	van der osten	lp: acanta 72.221792
gelobt)		cd: symposium 1227-1228
strauss	unnamed conductor	hmv/grammophon 65239/D 1002/
rosenkavalier	nast	043183
excerpt	van der osten	cd: symposium 1227-1228
(ist ein traum)		

it cannot be conclusively proven that the rosenkavalier sessions in may and august 1911 with principals of the world premiere in dresden earlier that year actually employed dresden musicians; however they are included here because of the obvious connection; certain items from these sessions also issued on eterna lp 820 778 and 822 870

003/november 1923/grammophon sessions

strauss   **busch**   grammophon 62463/68515
der bürger
als edelmann
minuets in g and a

mozart   grammophon 65861/69614
le nozze di figaro
overture;
smetana
bartered bride
overture

suppé   grammophon 65862/69615
schöne galathea
overture

j.strauss   grammophon 65863/69616/B20176-20177
fledermaus
overture

weber   grammophon 65864/69617
aufforderung
zum tanz

gluck   grammophon 65865/69618/B20180-20181
orfeo ed euridice
dance of the
blessed spirits
john amans, flute soloist

mendelssohn   grammophon 65865/69619/B20180-20181
a midsummer
night's dream
scherzo

bizet   grammophon 65866/69619
carmen
act 3 entr'acte

OPERNHAUS

Sonntag, am 20. Februar 1927, Anfang ¹/₂8 Uhr

Außer Anrecht

Die Macht des Schicksals
(La forza del destino)

Oper in einem Vorspiel und drei Akten

Dem Italienischen des F. M. Piave frei nachgedichtet und für die deutsche Opernbühne bearbeitet von Franz Werfel

Musik von Giuseppe Verdi

Inszenierung: Alois Mora

Musikalische Leitung: Fritz Busch   Spielleitung: Georg Toller

Personen:

Der Marchese von Calatrava	Willy Bader
Donna Leonore di Vargas ⎱ seine Kinder	⎰ Meta Seinemeyer
Don Carlo di Vargas ⎰	⎱ Robert Burg
Alvaro, ein Mestize	Tino Pattiera
Der Pater Guardian	Ivar Andresen
Fra Melitone	Ludwig Ermold
Preziosilla, eine junge Wahrsagerin	Erna Andreae
Mastro Trabuco, Maultiertreiber	Heinrich Teßmer
Ein Alcalde	Robert Büssel
Ein Chirurgus der spanisch-italienischen Truppen	Paul Schöffler
Curra, Kammerzofe Leonorens	Elfriede Haberkorn
Laienbruder	Julius Puttlitz

Franziskaner-Mönche, Maultiertreiber, spanische und italienische Soldaten, spanisches Volk, Marketenderinnen und Lagerdirnen, Kriegsvertriebene, italienische Rekruten, Diener des Marchese von Calatrava

Das Vorspiel spielt in Sevilla, der erste und letzte Akt im Umkreis eines spanischen Franziskanerklosters, der zweite Akt in Italien im siebzehnten Jahrhundert

Einstudierung der Chöre: Karl Pembaur

Einstudierung der Tarantella im zweiten Akt: Ellen v. Cleve-Petz

Bühnenbild: Max Hasait und Arthur Pältz   Trachten: Leonhard Fanto

Nach dem ersten und zweiten Akt je eine längere Pause

Sämtliche Plätze müssen vor Beginn der Vorstellung eingenommen werden

Textbücher sind für 1,00 RM bei den Türschließern zu haben

Gekaufte Karten werden nur bei Änderung der Vorstellung zurückgenommen

Kassenöffnung ¹/₂7 Uhr

Einlaß ³/₄7 Uhr — Anfang ¹/₂8 Uhr — Ende ¹/₄11 Uhr

OPERNHAUS

Mittwoch, am 12. April 1922, Anfang 7 Uhr

4. Sinfonie-Konzert
Reihe A

Leitung: Generalmusikdirektor Fritz Busch

I.

SCHUBERT, Franz: Unvollendete Sinfonie (H-moll)
    Allegro moderato. Andante con moto

15 Minuten Pause

II.

BRUCKNER, Anton: 8. Sinfonie (C-moll)
    Allegro moderato
    Scherzo (Allegro moderato)
    Adagio (Feierlich langsam)
    Finale (Feierlich, nicht schleppend)

Sämtliche Plätze müssen vor Beginn des Konzerts eingenommen werden

Gekaufte Karten werden nur bei Aenderung der Vorstellung zurückgenommen

Ende gegen 9 Uhr

003/concluded

mozart	**busch**	grammophon 65866/65868/69619/
zauberflöte		69621/B20186-20187
march of the priests		

tchaikovsky   grammophon 65867/69620
casse noissette
overture

wagner   grammophon 65867/65947/69620
meistersinger
von nürnberg
act 3 prelude

mozart   grammophon 65868/69621/B20186-20187
symphony no 39
minuetto

004/1927-1928/semperoper/grammophon sessions

puccini turandot excerpt (ho una casa)	**busch** tessmer sigmund schöffler *sung in german*	grammophon 66429 lp: acanta 72.221792

puccini   **busch**   grammophon 66430
turandot   dresden opera
excerpt   chorus
(gravi enormi   *sung in german*
ed imponenti)

verdi   **busch**   grammophon 66431/B20722
la forza del   cd: symposium 1280
destino
overture

verdi   grammophon 66432
la forza del   cd: symposium 1280
destino
battaglia e
tarantella

005/october 1931/semperoper/reichsrundfunk

brahms   **busch**   cd: tahra TAH 324-327
symphony   *disc containing opening section of the symphony*
no 2   *being damaged, this section of music is replaced*
                                with the commercial (hmv) recording by busch and
                                the danish radio orchestra

006/1932/semperoper/newsreel film

wagner   **busch**   lp: brüder-busch-gesellschaft FB 101
tannhäuser   cd: tahra TAH 324-327
overture   vhs video: teldec 4509 950383
                            laserdisc: teldec 4509 950386

ROYAL OPERA HOUSE
COVENT GARDEN

Lessees — Royal Opera House Company, Limited.
Secretary and Business Manager — CHARLES A. BARRAND

WILFRID VAN WYCK presents the

DRESDEN OPERA COMPANY'S SEASON

Wednesday, November 4th, 1936, at 7.45

MOZART'S OPERA

DON JUAN
(DON GIOVANNI)

In German

Produced by HANS STROHBACH
and JOSEF GIELEN

Don Juan	MATTHIEU AHLERSMEYER
Der Komtur	KURT BÖHME
Donna Anna	MARTA FUCHS
Don Ottavio	MARTIN KREMER
Donna Elvira	MARGARETE TESCHEMACHER
Leporello	THEO HERRMANN
	(from the State Opera, Hamburg)
Masetto	ARNO SCHELLENBERG
Zerlina	MARIA CEBOTARI

Haushofmeister, Diener, Kammerfrauen, Bauern,
Bauerinnen, Spielleute

Conductor — Dr. KARL BÖHM

ROYAL OPERA HOUSE
COVENT GARDEN

Lessees - Royal Opera House Company, Limited.
Secretary and Business Manager - CHARLES A. BARRAND

WILFRID VAN WYCK presents the
DRESDEN OPERA COMPANY'S SEASON

OPENING NIGHT OF THE SEASON
Monday, November 2nd, 1936, at 7

RICHARD STRAUSS' OPERA
DER ROSENKAVALIER
In German

Comedy with Music, in Three Acts, by
HUGO VON HOFMANNSTHAL
Produced by HANS STROHBACH

Die Feldmarschallin Fürstin Werdenberg	MARTA FUCHS
Der Baron Ochs auf Lerchenau	LUDWIG ERMOLD
Octavian	MARTA ROHS
Herr von Faninal	ARNO SCHELLENBERG
Sophie von Faninal	MARIA CEBOTARI
Jungfer Marianne Leimetzerin	WALBURGA VOGEL
Valzacchi	HANNS LANGE
Annina	HELENE JUNG
Ein Polizeikommissar	KURT BÖHME
Der Haushofmeister bei der Feldmarschallin	ROBERT BÜSSEL
Der Haushofmeister bei Faninal	HEINRICH TESSMER
Ein Notar	KURT BÖHME
Ein Wirt	HEINRICH TESSMER
Ein Sänger	MARTIN KREMER
Eine adelige Witwe	LUCIA DÖLITZSCH
Eine Modistin	ALICE LIEBESKIND
Ein Gelehrter	HANNS MEINERT
Ein Flötist	GINO NEPPACH
Ein Friseur	RUDOLF HORNUFF
Drei adelige Waisen	SUS. WAPNER-KÜHNE / LOTTE KRAUSE / LOTTE HIEKE
Ein Tierhändler	KLAUS HERMANNS
Conductor	KARL BÖHM

007/30 april 1935/berlin beethovensaal der philharmonie/electrola session

lortzing	**böhm**	78: electrola EH 916
zar und		lp: electrola SHZE 212
zimmermann		lp: emi 1C047 28555/1C151 30641-30642/
holzschuhtanz		1C137 53504-53507M
		cd: toshiba shinseido SGR 1205-1208
lortzing		78: electrola EH 916
undine		lp: emi 1C137 53505-53507M
ballet music		cd: toshiba shinseido SGR 1205-1208
beethoven		78: electrola EH 919
egmont		78: hmv C 2780
overture		lp: emi 1C137 53500-53504M
		cd: toshiba shinseido SGR 1201-1204

008/9-11 june 1936/semperoper/electrola sessions

bruckner	**böhm**	78: electrola DB 4450-4457
symphony		lp: emi 1C053 28924M/1C137 53508-53513M
no 4		cd: toshiba shinseido SGR 1209-1212
"romantic"		cd: zyx music PD 50132
		cd: dutton CDEA 5007
		cd: emi CHS 566 2062

008a/1936/semperoper/newsreel film

strauss	**böhm**	unpublished video recording
rosenkavalier	fuchs	
excerpt	rohs	
(hab' mir's	cebotari	
gelobt)		

009/7 november 1936/london queen's hall/bbc transcription

strauss	**strauss**	cd: appian APR 5527
don quixote	hesse	

georg seifert, viola soloist

strauss	**strauss**	cd: appian APR 5527
till eulenspiegels		*recording incomplete: surviving portion breaks*
lustige streiche		*off after figure 24 bar 4*

jan dahmen, violin soloist

010/31 may 1937/semperoper/electrola sessions

reger	**böhm**	78: electrola DB 4480-4483/
variations and		DB 8345-8348 auto
fugue on a		lp: emi 1C137 53508-53513M
theme of		cd: toshiba shinseido SGR 1209-1212
mozart		cd: zyx music PD 50122

011/1-3 june 1937/semperoper/electrola sessions

bruckner	**böhm**	78: electrola DB 4486-4494
symphony		lp: emi 1C137 53508-53513M
no 5		lp: discocorp IGI 452
		cd: toshiba shinseido SGR 1209-1212
		cd: zyx music PD 50142
		cd: emi CHS 566 2062

012/20-23 june 1938/semperoper/electrola sessions

wagner	**böhm**	78: electrola DB 4562-4576/
meistersinger	dresden opera	DB 8643-8657 auto
von nürnberg	chorus	lp: electrola E 80983-80984
act 3	teschemacher	lp: emi 1C137 53514-53517M
	jung	cd: pearl GEMMCDS 9121
	ralf	cd: preiser 89236
	kremer	cd: toshiba shinseido SGR 1213-1214
	nissen	*excerpts*
	s.nilsson	lp: electrola E 83387-83388
	fuchs	lp: emi 1C181 30665-30678M/
		1C187 29225-29226M

emi archive indicates that it was intended to complete this recording in dresden with acts 1 and 2 of the opera: a plan which was not fulfilled

Opernhaus

Sonnabend, am 30. September 1939, Anfang 5½ Uhr
2. Vorstellung für Donnerstag-Anrecht A vom 28. September
In neuer Einstudierung und Inszenierung

Die Meistersinger von Nürnberg

In drei Akten von Richard Wagner

Musikalische Leitung: Karl Böhm
Inszenierung: Heinz Arnold

Personen:

Hans Sachs, Schuster		Josef Herrmann
Veit Pogner, Goldschmied		Sven Nilsson
Kunz Vogelgesang, Kürschner		Willy Treffner
Konrad Nachtigall, Spengler		Robert Büssel
Sixtus Beckmesser, Stadtschreiber		Walter Streckfuß a. G.
Fritz Kothner, Bäcker	Meister-	Arno Schellenberg
Balthasar Zorn, Zinngießer	singer	Ludwig Eybisch
Ulrich Eißlinger, Würzkrämer		Heinrich Tessmer
Augustin Moser, Schneider		Hanns Lange
Hermann Ortel, Seifensieder		Jan Rittel
Hans Schwarz, Strumpfwirker		Hermann Greiner
Hans Foltz, Kupferschmied		Hermann Blasig
Walter von Stolzing, ein junger Ritter aus Franken		Torsten Ralf
David, Sachs' Lehrbube		Martin Kremer
Eva, Pogners Tochter		Margarete Teschemacher
Magdalene, Evas Amme		Inger Karén
Ein Nachtwächter		Robert Büssel

Bürger und Frauen aller Zünfte, Gesellen, Lehrbuben, Mädchen, Volk
Nürnberg um die Mitte des 16. Jahrhunderts

Einstudierung der Chöre: Ernst Hintze

Einstudierung des Tanzes: Valeria Kratina

Bühnenbild: Adolf Mahnke

Einrichtung: Georg Brandt — Trachten: Leonhard Fanto

013/24 june 1938/semperoper/electrola sessions

strauss	**böhm**	78: electrola DB 4557
rosenkavalier		lp: emi 1C137 53514-53519M
act 3 waltzes		cd: toshiba shinseido SGR 1213-1214
		cd: palladio PD 4119-4120
		cd: grammofono AB 78734-78735

reznicek
donna diana
overture

78: electrola DB 4560
lp: emi 1C137 53514-53519M
cd: toshiba shinseido SGR 1213-1214
cd: palladio PD 4119-4120
cd: grammofono AB 78734-78735

j.strauss
1001 nacht
intermezzo

78: electrola DB 4560
lp: emi 1C137 53514-53519M/
    1C147 30226-30227M
cd: toshiba shinseido SGR 1213-1214
cd: palladio PD 4119-4120
cd: grammofono AB 78734-78735
cd: preiser 90090

leoncavallo
i pagliacci
intermezzo

78: electrola DB 4556
45: hmv 7R 158
lp: emi 1C137 53514-53519M
cd: toshiba shinseido SGR 1213-1214
cd: iron needle IN 1311
cd: grammofono AB 78734-78735

mascagni
cavalleria
rusticana
intermezzo

78: electrola DB 4556
45: hmv 7R 158
lp: emi 1C137 53514-53519M
cd: toshiba shinseido SGR 1213-1214
cd: palladio PD 4119-4120
cd: iron needle IN 1311
cd: grammofono AB 78734-78735

014/25-28 june 1938/semperoper/electrola sessions

brahms	böhm	78: electrola DA 4443
hungarian		lp: emi 1C137 53505-53507M
dances nos		cd: toshiba shinseido SGR 1205-1208
5 and 6		

beethoven 78: electrola DB 4558-4559
leonore no 3 lp: emi 1C137 53500-53504M
overture cd: toshiba shinseido SGR 1201-1204

weber 78: electrola DB 4561
der freischütz lp: emi 1C137 53514-53519M
overture cd: toshiba shinseido SGR 1213-1214
cd: palladio PD 4119-4120
cd: iron needle IN 1311
cd: grammofono AB 78734-78735

mozart 78: electrola DB 4548-4549
eine kleine lp: emi 1C137 53500-53504M
nachtmusik cd: toshiba shinseido SGR 1201-1204

mozart **böhm** 78: electrola DB 4578-4581
violin concerto dahmen lp: emi 1C137 53500-53504M
no 3 cd: toshiba shinseido SGR 1201-1204

014a/january 1939/semperoper/electrola session
leoncavallo **böhm** electrola unpublished
i pagliacci ahlersmeyer
excerpt *sung in german*
(si puo?);
verdi
macbeth
excerpt
(pieta rispetto
amore)

015/3 january 1939/semperoper/columbia session

beethoven	**böhm**	78: columbia LX 847-850/LX 8462-8465 auto
piano concerto	gieseking	78: columbia (germany) LWX 288-291
no 4		78: columbia (france) LFX 709-712

78: columbia (usa) M 411
lp: emi 1C137 53500-53504M/
    3C153 52700-52705M
lp: discocorp RR 415
cd: toshiba shinseido SGR 1201-1204
cd: grammofono AB 78506
cd: appian APR 5512
cd: radio years RY 61

016/january 1939/semperoper/electrola sessions

tchaikovsky	**böhm**	78: electrola DB 4632
capriccio		lp: emi 1C137 53505-53507M
italien		cd: toshiba shinseido SGR 1205-1208
abridged		

strauss		78: electrola DB 4639
salome		lp: emi 1C137 53514-53519M
dance of the		lp: acanta DE 23280-23281
7 veils		cd: toshiba shinseido SGR 1213-1214
		cd: palladio PD 4119-4120
		cd: grammofono AB 78734-78735

strauss	**böhm**	78: electrola DB 4627
daphne	teschemacher	lp: emi 1C137 53514-53519M
excerpt		cd: toshiba shinseido SGR 1213-1214
(wind spiele		cd: preiser 89049/89090
mit mir!)		

strauss		78: electrola DB 4628
daphne		lp: emi 1C137 53514-53519M/EX 29 01693
excerpt		lp: acanta DE 23280-23281
(o wie gerne		cd: toshiba shinseido SGR 1213-1214
blieb' ich		cd: preiser 89049/89090
bei dir!)		cd: testament SBT 0132

016/concluded

strauss	**böhm**	78: electrola DB 4628
daphne	ralf	lp: emi 1C137 53514-53519M
excerpt		lp: rococo 5233
(götter! brüder		lp: acanta DE 23280-23281
im hohen olymp!)		cd: toshiba shinseido SGR 1213-1214
		cd: preiser 89077

these scenes from daphne were recorded with the principals of the dresden premiere of the opera, which had taken place on 15 october 1938

strauss	**böhm**	78: electrola DB 4625-4626
don juan		lp: emi 1C137 53508-53513M
		cd: toshiba shinseido SGR 1209-1212
		cd: dutton CDEA 5007

humperdinck	78: electrola DB 4648
hänsel und	lp: emi 1C137 53514-53519M
gretel	cd: toshiba shinseido SGR 1213-1214
overture	cd: palladio PD 4119-4120
	cd: grammofono AB 78734-78735

j.strauss	78: electrola DB 4638
die fledermaus	lp: emi 1C137 53514-53519M
overture	cd: toshiba shinseido SGR 1213-1214
	cd: palladio PD 4119-4120
	cd: grammofono AB 78734-78735
	cd: tahra TAH 358-361

wagner	**böhm**	78: electrola DA 4456
lohengrin	dresden opera	lp: emi 1C137 53514-53519M
excerpt	chorus	cd: toshiba shinseido SGR 1213-1214
(treulich geführt)		

weber	78: electrola DA 4457
der freischütz	lp: emi 1C137 53514-53519M
excerpt	cd: toshiba shinseido SGR 1213-1214
(was gleicht wohl	
auf erden)	

gounod	**böhm**	78: electrola DA 4457
faust	dresden opera	lp: emi 1C137 53514-53519M
excerpt	chorus	cd: toshiba shinseido SGR 1213-1214
(gloire	*sung in german*	
immortelle!)		

017/june 1939/semperoper/electrola sessions

brahms piano concerto no 2 *karl hesse, cello soloist*	**böhm** backhaus	78: electrola DB 5500-5505 lp: emi 1C053 01362M/2C051 01362M/ 1C137 53505-53507M lp: toshiba GR 2098 cd: toshiba shinseido SGR 1205-1208 cd: memories HR 4442-4443 cd: biddulph LWH 018
beethoven piano concerto no 3	**böhm** kolessa	78: electrola DB 5506-5510 lp: emi 1C137 53500-53504M cd: toshiba shinseido SGR 1201-1204 cd: iron needle IN 1381
mozart entführung aus dem serail; le nozze di figaro overtures	**böhm**	78: electrola DB 4692 lp: emi 1C137 53514-53519M cd: toshiba shinseido SGR 1213-1214 cd: palladio PD 4119-4120 cd: iron needle IN 1311 cd: grammofono AB 78734-78735
brahms symphony no 4		78: electrola DB 4684-4689/ DB 8776-8781 auto lp: emi 1C137 53508-53513M cd: toshiba shinseido SGR 1209-1212 cd: zyx music PD 50122 cd: dutton CDEA 5006
wagner meistersinger von nürnberg overture		78: electrola DB 4698 lp: emi 1C137 53514-53519M cd: toshiba shindeido SGR 1213-1214 cd: palladio PD 4119-4120 cd: iron needle IN 1311 cd: grammofono AB 78734-78735

018/26-28 june 1939/semperoper/electrola sessions
beethoven **böhm** 78: electrola DB 5511-5515
piano concerto fischer lp: emi 1C137 53500-53504M/
no 5 2C051 45660M
"emperor" lp: toshiba EAC 40216
cd: toshiba shindeido SGR 1201-1204
cd: dante HPC 007
cd: piano library PL 195

019/29-30 june 1939/semperoper/electrola sessions
beethoven **böhm** 78: electrola DB 5516-5520
violin strub lp: emi 1C137 53500-53504M
concerto cd: toshiba shinseido SGR 1201-1204

019a/1939/semperoper/reichsrundfunk recording
wagner **striegler** lp: acanta DE 23108-23109
der fliegende herrmann cd: pilz CD 78008
holländer *recording incomplete*
excerpt
(wie aus der ferne)

020/january 1940/semperoper/electrola sessions
wagner **böhm** 78: electrola DB 5555-5556
tannhäuser lp: emi 1C137 53514-53519M
overture cd: toshiba shinseido SGR 1213-1214
cd: palladio PD 4119-4120
cd: iron needle IN 1311
cd: grammofono AB 78734-78735

wagner 78: electrola DB 5553-5554
der fliegende lp: emi 1C137 53514-53519M
holländer cd: toshiba shinseido SGR 1213-1214
overture cd: palladio PD 4119-4120
cd: iron needle IN 1311
cd: grammofono AB 78734-78735

wagner 78: electrola DB 5554
lohengrin lp: emi 1C137 53514-53519M
act 3 prelude cd: toshiba shinseido SGR 1213-1214
cd: palladio PD 4119-4120
cd: iron needle IN 1311
cd: grammofono AB 78734-78735

021/january 1940/semperoper/electrola session

mascagni	**böhm**	78: electrola DB 5558
cavalleria	dresden opera	lp: emi 1C137 53514-53519M
rusticana	chorus	cd: toshiba shinseido SGR 2313-1214
excerpt	goltz	
(regina coeli)		

wagner **böhm** 78: electrola DB 5551
tannhäuser dresden opera lp: emi 1C137 53514-53519M
excerpt chorus cd: toshiba shinseido SGR 1213-1214
(freudig
begrüssen wir
die edle halle!);
lohengrin
excerpt
(gesegnet soll
sie schreiten)

022/january 1940/semperoper/electrola sessions
j.strauss **böhm** 78: electrola DB 5560
kaiserwalzer lp: emi 1C137 53514-53519M
cd: toshiba shinseido SGR 1213-1214
cd: palladio PD 4119-4120
cd: grammofono AB 78734-78735

weber 78: electrola DB 5557
oberon lp: emi 1C137 53514-53519M
overture cd: toshiba shinseido SGR 1213-1214
cd: palladio PD 4119-4120
cd: grammofono AB 78734-78735

verdi 78: electrola DB 5558
aida lp: emi 1C137 53514-53519M
prelude cd: toshiba shinseido SGR 1213-1214
cd: palladio PD 4119-4120
cd: iron needle IN 1311
cd: grammofono AB 78734-78735

smetana 78: electrola DB 5552
bartered bride lp: emi 1C137 53514-53519M
overture cd: toshiba shinseido SGR 1213-1214
cd: palladio PD 4119-4120
cd: grammofono AB 78734-78735

schubert 78: electrola DB 5559
marche militaire; lp: emi 1C137 53505-53507M
berlioz cd: toshiba shinseido SGR 1205-1208
marche hongroise/
la damnation
de faust

023/january 1940/semperoper/columbia sessions
brahms **böhm** 78: columbia (germany) LWX 331-335
violin schneiderhan lp: emi 1C137 53505-53507M
concerto cd: toshiba shinseido SGR 1205-1208

berger **böhm** 78: columbia (germany) LWX 335
rondino lp: emi 1C137 53508-53513M
giocoso cd: toshiba shinseido SGR 1209-1212
cd: zyx music PD 50152

023a/1940-1941/semperoper/electrola sessions

flotow martha excerpt (ach so fromm)	unnamed conductor treffner	78: electrola DB 5597 cd: preiser 89545

ponchielli unnamed 78: electrola DB 5597
la gioconda conductor cd: preiser 89545
excerpt treffner
(cielo e mar) *sung in german*

schmidseder unnamed 78: electrola EG 7204
die heimkehr conductor cd: preiser 89545
nach mittenwald treffner
excerpts
(an deinem herzen
ist meine heimat;
liebe kleine geige)

verdi unnamed 78: electrola DB 5647
otello excerpt conductor cd: preiser 89076
(credo in un herrmann
dio crudel) *sung in german*

024/11 january 1941/semperoper/electrola sessions

mozart	**böhm**	78: electrola DB 5628-5629
horn concerto	zimolong	lp: emi 1C137 53500-53504M
no 3		cd: toshiba shinseido SGR 1201-1204

puccini **böhm** 78: electrola DB 5620
la fanciulla ralf lp: emi 1C137 53514-53519M
del west *sung in german* lp: rococo 5233
excerpt cd: toshiba shinseido SGR 1213-1214
(ch'ella mi cd: preiser 89077
creda libero)

verdi **böhm** 78: electrola DB 5620
otello ralf lp: emi 1C137 53514-53519M
excerpt herrmann lp: rococo 5233
(si per ciel *sung in german* cd: toshiba shinseido SGR 1213-1214
marmoreo cd: iron needle IN 1311
giuro!) cd: preiser 89077
cd: hamburger archiv für gesangskunst
cd: grammofono AB 78734-78735

wagner **böhm** 78: electrola DB 5623
meistersinger herrmann lp: emi 1C137 53514-53519M
von nürnberg lp: preiser LV 49
excerpt cd: toshiba shinseido SGR 1213-1214
(was duftet doch cd: preiser 89076
der flieder)

025/january 1941/semperoper/electrola sessions

pfitzner symphony op 46	**böhm**	78: electrola DB 5618-5619 lp: electrola E 60802 lp: emi 1C137 53508-53513M cd: toshiba shinseido SGR 1209-1212 cd: zyx music PD 50152
strauss till eulenspiegels lustige streiche		78: electrola DB 5621-5622 lp: emi 1C137 53508-53513M cd: toshiba shinseido SGR 1209-1212 cd: zyx music PD 50152
strauss rosenkavalier excerpt (mit ihren augen voll tränen/ist ein traum)	**böhm** rethy höngen	78: electrola DB 5617 lp: emi 1C137 53514-53519M/EX 29 01313 cd: toshiba shinseido SGR 1312-1214 cd: preiser 89077
beethoven symphony no 9 "choral"	**böhm** dresden opera chorus teschemacher höngen ralf herrmann	78: electrola DB 5652-5660 lp: emi 1C137 53508-53513M cd: toshiba shinseido SGR 1209-1212 cd: zyx music PD 50112 cd: dante LYS 404

026/1942/semperoper/columbia session

schumann piano concerto	**böhm** gieseking	78: columbia (germany) LWX 356-359 lp: emi 1C137 53505-53507M cd: toshiba shinseido SGR 1205-1208

027/1942/semperoper/electrola session

marschner hans heiling excerpt (an jenem tag)	unnamed conductor herrmann	78: electrola DB 5678 cd: preiser 89076
weber der freischütz excerpt (hier im ird'schen jammertal)		78: electrola DA 4498 cd: preiser 89076

028/june 1942/semperoper/reichsrundfunk recordings

strauss arabella excerpt (er ist der richtige nicht)	**böhm** teschemacher goltz	lp: eterna 821 084 lp: acanta DE 23280-23281 cd: berlin classics BC 20492/BC 25002
strauss arabella excerpt (und du wirst mein gebieter sein)	**böhm** teschemacher ahlersmayer	lp: acanta DE 23280-23281 cd: berlin classics BC 20492/BC 25002
strauss arabella excerpt (das war sehr gut mandryka)		lp: eterna 821 084 lp: acanta DE 23280-23281/22.214881
strauss die frau ohne schatten zwischenspiel from act 1	**böhm**	lp: acanta DE 23280-23281
strauss die frau ohne schatten excerpt (sie haben es mir gesagt)	**böhm** herrmann	lp: acanta 72.221792/DE 23108-23109/ DE 23280-23281
strauss die frau ohne schatten excerpt (falke du wiedergefundener) *karl hesse, cello soloist*	**böhm** ralf	lp: eterna 820 933 lp: acanta DE 23280-23281 cd: berlin classics BC20492/BC25002/BC 93942 cd: preiser 89077

029/12 june 1942/semperoper/reichsrundfunk recording
schubert   **böhm**   lp: discocorp IGI 365
symphony   cd: fonoteam CD 74808
no 5   cd: tahra TAH 324-327

030/26 november 1942/semperoper/reichsrundfunk recordings
francaix   **striegler**   lp: urania URLP 7122
le roi nu
suite from
the ballet

verdi   **striegler**   lp: eterna 820 960/822 671-672
otello   herrmann   lp: acanta DE 23108-23109
excerpt   *sung in german*   cd: hamburger archiv für gesangskunst
(credo in un
dio crudel!)

wagner   **striegler**   lp: acanta DE 23108-23109
meistersinger   herrmann   cd: hamburger archiv für gesangskunst
von nürnberg
excerpt
(was duftet doch
der flieder)

031/30 november 1942/semperoper/reichsrundfunk recording
pfitzner   **böhm**   lp: urania URLP 7044
symphony   cd: fonoteam CD 74808
op 46

032/4-5 december 1942/semperoper/reichsrundfunk recording

bizet	**böhm**	cd: preiser 90152
carmen	dresden opera	cd: cantus classics CACD 500022
	chorus	*excerpts*
	höngen	lp: eterna 820 933/820 960
	weidlich	lp: acanta 10.21362/BB 21362/
	ralf	72.221792/DE 23108-23109
	herrmann	cd: berlin classics BC 20492
	sung in german	cd: cantus classics CACD 500028
		cd: hamburger archiv für gesangskunst

033/2 march 1943/semperoper/reichsrundfunk recordings

dvorak	**elmendorff**	lp: eterna
the jacobin	teschemacher	cd: preiser 90182
excerpt	s.nilsson	
(sleep my	*sung in german*	
child!)		

dvorak	**elmendorff**	lp: acanta 22.223159
the jacobin	trötschel	cd: preiser 89520
excerpr	fehenberger	
(autumn has	*sung in german*	
passed)		

dvorak		lp: acanta 22.223159
the jacobin		
excerpt		
(let me speak		
to you!)		

mozart	**elmendorff**	lp: acanta 72.221792
le nozze di	düren	
figaro	herrmann	
excerpt	*sung in german*	
(cinque dieci!)		

wagner	**elmendorff**	lp: acanta 22.226379
der engel;	teschemacher	
im treibhaus/		
wesendonk-lieder		

033a/1943/semperoper/electrola sessions

wagner	**elmendorff**	cd: preiser 89076
das rheingold	herrmann	*unpublished electrola 78rpm recording*
(abendlich strahlt)		

wagner
die walküre excerpt
(leb wohl du kühnes herrliches kind)

78: electrola DB 7675-7676
cd: preiser 89076

wagner
der fliegende holländer excerpt
(die frist ist um)

78: electrola DB 7645
cd: preiser 89076

mozart **elmendorff** cd: preiser 89545
cosi fan tutte treffner *unpublished electrola 78rpm recordings*
excerpt *sung in german*
(un aura amorosa);
donizetti
la favorita excerpt
(una vergine)

verdi **elmendorff** cd: preiser 89545
messa da treffner *unpublished electrola 78rpm recordings*
requiem excerpt
(ingemisco);
haydn
die jahreszeiten excerpt
(dem druck erlieget die natur)

dostal
manina excerpts
(ich such' in jeder frau; kurz ist der mai)

78: electrola EG 7289
cd: preiser 89545

033a/continued

flotow martha excerpt (blickt sein auge doch so ehrlich); cornelius der barbier von bagdad excerpt (o holdes bild!); lehar giuditta excerpt (schön wie die blaue sommernacht); igelhoff eine nacht mit rosita excerpt die erste grosse lieb')	**elmendorff** teschemacher treffner	cd: preiser 89545 *unpublished electrola 78rpm recordings*
weber peter schmoll excerpt (ja gottes erde ist schön)	**elmendorff** herrmann	cd: preiser 89076 *unpublished electrola 78rpm recording*
leoncavallo i pagliacci excerpt (so ben che difforme)	**elmendorff** düren herrmann *sung in german*	cd: preiser 89076 *unpublished electrola 78rpm recording*

033a/concluded
lehar **elmendorff** cd: preiser 89545
der graf von düren *unpublished electrola 78rpm recordings*
luxemburg treffner
excerpts
(lieber freund;
nur geduld)

wagner **elmendorff** cd: preiser 89076
der fliegende herrmann *unpublished electrola 78rpm recordings*
holländer böhme
excerpt
(durch sturm und
tosend wind);
beethoven
fidelio excerpt
(jetzt alter hat
es eile!)

verdi **elmendorff** 78: electrola DB 7700
otello excerpt treffner cd: preiser 89076/89545
(roderigo herrmann
beviam!) tessmer
 sung in german

the orchestra was not actually named on these 1943 electrola recordings

SÄCHSISCHE STAATSTHEATER DRESDEN
OPERNHAUS

Sonnabend, am 4. Dezember 1943, Anfang 4½ Uhr

Außer Anrecht

In der neuen Einstudierung und Inszenierung

Der Widerspenstigen Zähmung

Komische Oper in vier Akten

Text frei nach Shakespeares gleichnamigem Lustspiel von J. V. Widmann

Musik von Hermann Goetz

Musikalische Leitung: Karl Elmendorff

Inszenierung: Max Hofmüller

Personen:

Baptista, ein reicher Edelmann in Padua	Sven Nilsson
Katharina ⎫ seine Töchter	Margarete Teschemacher
Bianca ⎭	Elfride Trötschel
Hortensio ⎫ Biancas Freier	Heinrich Pflanzl
Lucentio ⎭	Pavel Mirov
Petrucchio, ein Edelmann aus Verona	Mathieu Ahlersmeyer
Grumio, sein Diener	Hans Löbel
Ein Schneider	Karl Wessely
Eine Witwe	Ina Arowska
Haushofmeister	Jakob Velder
Haushälterin	Edith Dietrich

Nachbarn, Gäste, Diener

Schauplatz: 1. Akt: Vor Baptistas Haus in Padua
2. Akt: Zimmer in Baptistas Haus
3. Akt: Saal in Baptistas Haus
4. Akt: Zimmer in Petrucchios Landhaus

Chöre: Ernst Hintze

Bühnenbild und Trachten: Richard Panzer

Technische Einrichtung: Georg Brandt

Pause nach dem zweiten Akt

034/22 november 1943/semperoper/reichsrundfunk recording

goetz	**elmendorff**	cd: preiser 90416
der	dresden opera	cd: cantus classics CACD 500066
widerspenstigen	chorus	*excerpts*
zähmung	teschemacher	lp: acanta 72.221792/22.221210/
	trötschel	22.214885
	mirov	cd: myto HO 57
	ahlersmayer	*recording completed in december 1943 and*
	s.nilsson	*january 1944*
	frick	

034a/5 february 1944/semperoper/newsreel film

von einem	**elmendorff**	unpublished video fragment
prinzessin		
turandot ballet		

035/1944/semperoper/reichsrundfunk recordings

lortzing	**striegler**	lp: acanta 22.223159
der wildschütz	dresden opera	
excerpt	chorus	
(duet baculus-	trötschel	
gretchen)	pflanzl	

strauss	**striegler**	lp: acanta 22.226948
salome	goltz	
excerpt	schöffler	
(wird dir		
nicht bange?)		

verdi	**striegler**	lp: eterna 821 084
la forza del	teschemacher	
destino	*sung in german*	
excerpt		
(pace pace!)		

mozart	**striegler**	lp: acanta 22.226948
le nozze di	schöffler	
figaro	*sung in german*	
excerpt		
(hai gia vinta		
la causa!)		

036/1944/semperoper/reichsrundfunk recordings

rossini	**striegler**	lp: acanta BB 23103
il barbiere	dresden opera	
di siviglia	chorus	
excerpts	reichelt	
(lieto ridente;	hofer-sterkel	
arditi all'ire;	fehenberger	
una voce	löbel	
poco fa;	schellenberg	
a un dottor;	frick	
ehi di casa!)	böhme	
	sung in german	

orff	**striegler**	78: grammophon LM 68 151
die kluge	fehenberger	45: dg NL 32219
excerpts	löbel	*conductor incorrectly described by john hunt in*
(o hätt' ich	frick	*conductors on the yellow label as eugen jochum*
meiner tochter	böhme	
nur geglaubt;		
als die treue		
ward geboren)		

037/1944/semperoper/reichsrundfunk recording

verdi	**elmendorff**	lp: preiser LM 11
luisa miller	dresden opera	cd: preiser 90055
	chorus	*excerpts*
	cebotari	lp: eterna 820 183/822 870-871
	rott	lp: historia H 677-678
	trötschel	lp: acanta 72.221792/22.21805/22.22028/
	hopf	22.21483-21484/DE 23108-23109
	herrmann	lp: artiphon ART 209
	böhme	cd: pilz CD 78008
	hann	
	sung in german	

038/1944/semperoper/reichsrundfunk recordings

mozart entführung aus dem serail excerpt (o wie ängstlich)	**elmendorff** fehenberger	cd: pilz CD 78008
mozart don giovanni excerpt (deh vieni alla finestra)	**elmendorff** schöffler *sung in german*	lp: acanta 22.226948
weber euryanthe excerpt (kein schlaf gibt meinem wilden blute ruh')	**elmendorff** herrmann	lp: eterna 820 960/821 872 lp: acanta DE 23108-23109 cd: berlin classics BC 20492 cd: hamburger archiv für gesangskunst
wagner siegfried excerpt (auf wolkigen höh'n wohnen die götter)		lp: acanta DE 23108-23109/40.23502 cd: hamburger archiv für gesangskunst
wagner götter- dämmerung excerpt (blühenden lebens labende glut!)	**elmendorff** lorenz herrmann	lp: acanta DE 23108-23109 *acanta describes conductor as striegler*

039/1 june 1944/semperoper/reichsrundfunk recording

weber	**elmendorff**	cd: preiser 90386
der freischütz	dresden opera	*excerpts*
	chorus	lp: eterna 821 084
	teschemacher	lp: acanta 72.221792/22.220281/
	trötschel	22.223159
	fehenberger	cd: berlin classics BC 20492
	böhme	
	pflanzl	
	s.nilsson	
	schellenberg	

040/20 june 1944/semperoper/reichsrundfunk recording

mozart	**elmendorff**	lp: eterna 820 238-820 240
don giovanni	dresden opera	lp: dg LPEM 19 250-19 252
	chorus	cd: berlin classics 0325 001
	schech	*excerpts*
	teschemacher	lp: eterna 820 238
	weidlich	lp: acanta DE 23059
	hopf	cd: berlin classics BC 93942
	ahlersmayer	
	böhme	
	pflanzl	
	frick	
	sung in german	

041/3 august 1944/steinsaal des hygienemuseums/reichsrundfunk recording

schubert	**elmendorff**	lp: melodiya M10 46117 007
symphony		cd: tahra TAH 324-327
no 4		
"tragic"		
beethoven		lp: melodiya M10 46117 007
grosse fuge		

PERFORMING ART * ИСПОЛНИТЕЛЬСКОЕ ИСКУССТВО

DRESDEN STAATSKAPELLE
Conductor
Karl ELMENDORFF

F. SCHUBERT   L. BEETHOVEN
Symphony No. 4   Grosse Fuge

ДРЕЗДЕНСКАЯ
ГОСУДАРСТВЕННАЯ КАПЕЛЛА
Дирижер
Карл ЭЛЬМЕНДОРФ

Ф. ШУБЕРТ   Л. БЕТХОВЕН
Симфония № 4   Большая фуга

042/21 september 1944/steinsaal des hygienemuseums/reichsrundfunk recordings

beethoven	**elmendorff**	lp: eterna 822 871
fidelio	fehenberger	cd: preiser 89520
excerpt		
(gott welch		
dunkel hier!/		
in des lebens		
frühlingstagen)		

wagner	**elmendorff**	lp: eterna 822 871
tannhäuser	schech	
excerpt		
(dich teure halle!)		

wagner	**elmendorff**	lp: eterna 820 960
die walküre	herrmann	lp: preiser 0120 015-016
excerpt		lp: acanta DE 23108-23109/40.23502
(leb wohl du		cd: tahta TAH 324-327
herrliches kind!)		cd: hamburger archiv für gesangskunst

wagner	**elmendorff**	lp: preiser 0120 015-016
die walküre	teschemacher	cd: preiser 90015
act 1	lorenz	cd: tahra TAH 324-327
	böhme	*excerpts*
		lp: acanta 22.220281
		cd: phonographe PHC 5016-5017

043/14-16 november 1944/steinsaal des hygienemuseums/ reichsrundfunk recording

auber	**elmendorff**	lp: acanta 22.292691
fra diavolo	dresden opera	cd: preiser 90349
	chorus	
	schilp	
	beilke	
	hopf	
	fehenberger	
	schellenberg	
	frick	
	böhme	
	sung in german	

044/28 november 1944/steinsaal des hygienemuseums/reichsrundfunk recording

brahms	**elmendorff**	unpublished radio broadcast
symphony		*recording incomplete*
no 4		

045/11 december 1944/steinsaal des hygienemuseums/reichsrundfunk recording

von einem	**elmendorff**	78: grammophon LM 68 186-188/
konzert für		LM 69 488-489
orchester		

046/21-28 december 1944/semperoper/reichsrundfunk recording

wolf	**elmendorff**	lp: urania URLP 208
der corregidor	dresden opera	lp: acanta 30.214087
	chorus	cd: preiser 90182
	teschemacher	*excerpts*
	fuchs	lp: eterna 820 960
	rott	lp: acanta DE 23108-23109
	erb	cd: hamburger archiv für gesangskunst
	herrmann	
	böhme	
	hann	
	frick	

047/january 1945/steinsaal des hygienemuseums/reichsrundfunk recording

loewe	**striegler**	unpublished radio broadcast
hochzeitslied;	herrmann	*these items appear in a discography of josef herrmann*
heinrich		*published in the series stimmen die um die welt gingen*
der vogler;		*(münster 1999); as they have not been published it*
wolf		*cannot be verified if the sächsische staatskapelle*
der könig bei der		*actually participates; wolf item is dated october 1944*
krönung		

048/1946/grosser sendesaal des hygienemuseums/mitteldeutscher rundfunk

beethoven	**striegler**	lp: acanta DE 23059
fidelio	dresden opera	*this recital lp also includes an aria from*
excerpt	chorus	*mascagni cavalleria rusticana incorrectly*
(gott welch	hopf	*attributed to dresden but actually recorded in*
dunkel hier!/	*italian items*	*berlin; il trovatore item is incorrectly dated 1948;*
in des lebens	*sung in german*	*andrea chenier item is also re-issued on cd by*
frühlingstagen);		*pilz CD 78008*

giordano
andrea chenier
excerpt
(un di al'
azurro spazio);
leoncavallo
i pagliacci
excerpts
(testa adorata;
vesti la giubba);
puccini
tosca
excerpt
(e lucevan
le stelle);
turandot
excerpts
(non piangere liu;
nessun dorma);
verdi
il trovatore
excerpt
(di quella pira);
wagner
lohengrin
excerpts
(atmest du nicht
die süssen düfte;
in fernem land)

joseph keilberth, generalmusikdirektor 1945-1950

STAATSOPER DRESDEN

Montag, den 20. September 1948, 17 Uhr
im Großen Haus der Staatstheater Dresden

Generalprobe zur neuen Einstudierung und Inszenierung
Für Mitarbeiter am Neubau des Großen Hauses

FIDELIO

Oper in zwei Akten von J. Sonnleithner und G. F. Treitschke

Musik von Ludwig van Beethoven

Musikalische Leitung: Joseph Keilberth · Inszenierung: Heinz Arnold

Gesamtausstattung: Karl von Appen

Personen:

Don Fernando, Minister	Heinrich Pflanzl
Don Pizarro, Gouverneur eines Staatsgefängnisses	Josef Herrmann
Florestan, ein Gefangener	Bernd Aldenhoff
Leonore, seine Gemahlin, unter dem Namen Fidelio	Christel Goltz
Rocco, Kerkermeister	Gottlob Frick
Marcelline, seine Tochter	Elfride Trötschel
Jaquino, Pförtner	Erich Zimmermann
Erster Gefangener	Horst Weber
Zweiter Gefangener	Werner Faulhaber

Chöre, einstudiert von Ernst Hintze, ausgeführt vom Opernchor, im Schlußchor verstärkt durch den Sinfoniechor und den Chor der Staatlichen Akademie für Musik und Theater

049/1 january 1948/grosser sendesaal des hygienemuseums/
mitteldeutscher rundfunk

wagner	**wehding**	unpublished radio broadcast
meistersinger	dresden opera	
von nürnberg	chorus	
excerpt	herrmann	
(wach auf		
chor)		

050/20 may 1948/grosser sendesaal des hygienemuseums/mitteldeutscher
rundfunk

strauss	**keilberth**	lp: eterna 822 868-869
salome	goltz	lp: olympic (usa) 9101
	karen	lp: oceanic (usa) 302
	lange	lp: musical treasures (usa) 2027
	aldenhoff	cd: berlin classics BC 20622
	dittrich	*excerpts*
	herrmann	lp: eterna 822 671-672/827 870-871
		lp: acanta 72.221792/DE 23108-23109
		cd: berlin classics BC 93942/preiser 89523
		josef herrmann discography (münster 1999) mentions mitteldeutscher rundfunk broadcast of the scene "wo ist er dessen sündenbecher jetzt voll ist" on 4 february 1949 with goltz, dittrich and herrmann: it is assumed that this was taken from the complete broadcast recording of 20 may 1948

051/22 september 1948/schauspielhaus/mitteldeutscher rundfunk

beethoven	**keilberth**	unpublished radio broadcast
fidelio	dresden opera	*tapes of this complete performance of the re-opening of*
	chorus	*sächsische staatsoper's temporary home seem to be*
	goltz	*irretrievably lost but the following sections have*
	trötschel	*survived :-*
	aldenhoff	*ha welch ein augenblick!*
	zimmermann	lp: eterna 820 960
	pflanzl	lp: acanta DE 23108-23109
	herrmann	cd: berlin classics BC 20492/0125 002
	frick	cd: hamburger archiv für gesangskunst
		gott welch dunkel hier/in des lebens frühlingstagen
		cd: tahra TAH 324-327
		cd: preiser 89523
		o namenlose freude!
		lp: acanta 72.221792
		cd: preiser 89523
		heil sei dem tag!
		unpublished newsreel film fragment

052/december 1948/steinsaal des hygienemuseums/mitteldeutscher rundfunk

dvorak	**keilberth**	lp: urania URLP 219/US 5219
rusalka	dresden opera	*excerpts*
	chorus	lp: acanta 72.221792
	trötschel	*in the notes to tahra CD collection "tribute to the*
	otto	*staatskapelle of dresden" (TAH 324-327) rené*
	lange	*trémine mentions a recording date for this opera*
	rott	*of 28 august 1949: this is probably the date on*
	schindler	*which the recording was broadcast*
	zimmermann	
	frick	
	sung in german	

053/may 1949/sendersaal des hygienemuseums/mitteldeutscher rundfunk

bizet	**löwlein**	lp: acanta 22.223159
carmen	trötschel	
excerpt	sauerbaum	
(parle-moi	*sung in german*	
de ma mere!)		

janacek	**richter**	lp: acanta 22.223159
kata	trötschel	
kabanova	gossmann	
excerpt	*sung in german*	
(guess what		
occurred		
to me?)		

054/22 december 1949/sendersaal des hygienemuseums/mitteldeutscher rundfunk

mozart	**kempe**	cd: tahra TAH 324-327
cosi fan		
tutte		
overture		

wagner		cd: tahra TAH 324-327/TAH 370-371
lohengrin		
prelude		

054/concluded
mozart   **kempe**   lp: eterna 822 871
zauberflöte   otto
excerpt   schellenberg
(papagena!
papageno!)

strauss   **kempe**   lp: acanta 22.220281
rosenkavalier   dresden opera
excerpt   chorus
(da lieg' ich)   rott
                  böhme

donizetti   **kempe**   lp: acanta 22.220281
don pasquale   schellenberg
excerpt   böhme
(cheti cheti   *sung in german*
immantinente)

mussorgsky   **kempe**   cd: pilz CD 78008
boris   otto
godunov   rott
excerpt   *sung in german*
(once a gnat
was sawing wood)

wagner   **kempe**   cd: pilz CD 78008
tannhäuser   paul
excerpt
(wie todesahnung/
o du mein holder
abendstern)

meyerbeer   **kempe**   cd: preiser 89523
l'africaine   aldenhoff   *orchestra and conductor incorrectly described*
excerpt   *sung in german*   *leipzig radio orchestra and rolf kleinert*
(o paradis!)

055/20 may 1950/sendesaal des hygienemuseums/mitteldeutscher rundfunk

tchaikovsky	**kempe**	cd: pilz CD 78008
evgeny	frick	
onegin	*sung in german*	
excerpt		
(everyone		
knows love on		
earth)		

verdi	**kempe**	cd: pilz CD 78008
la forza del	goltz	
destino	*sung in german*	
excerpt		
(pace pace!)		

056/1 december 1950/sendesaal des hygienemuseums/mitteldeutscher rundfunk

schubert	**kempe**	cd: tahra TAH 370-371
symphony		
no 9		
"great"		

057/7 december 1950/sendesaal des hygienemuseums/mitteldeutscher rundfunk

mozart	**kempe**	cd: pilz CD 78008
don giovanni	trötschel	
excerpt	löbel	
(la ci darem	*sung in german*	
la mano)		

058/21-23 december 1950/steinsaal des hygienemuseums/mitteldeutscher rundfunk

strauss	**kempe**	lp: urania URLP 210/URLP 9201
rosenkavalier	dresden opera	lp: nixa 52014
	chorus	*excerpts*
	bäumer	lp: urania 602/7062/8010/9602/58010
	richter	lp: saga XID 5177
	lemnitz	lp: historia H 704-705
	böhme	
	löbel	

059/20 april 1951/sendesaal des hygienemuseums/mitteldeutscher rundfunk

puccini	**löwlein**	lp: acanta 22.223159
madama	trötschel	
butterfly	sauerbaum	
excerpt	*sung in german*	
(bimba dagli		
occhi)		

060/29 april-2 may 1951/steinsaal des hygienemuseums/mitteldeutscher rundfunk

wagner	**kempe**	lp: urania URLP 206
meistersinger	dresden opera	lp: vox OPBX 141
von nürnberg	chorus	lp: acanta 22.292673
	lemnitz	cd: myto MCD 961138
	walter-sacks	*excerpts*
	aldenhoff	lp: urania 7067/7077
	unger	lp: vox OPL 350/PL 15100
	frantz	lp: saga XID 5117/XID 5290/STXID 5290
	böhme	lp: acanta DE 29269
	pflanzl	lp: world records T 295

WAGNER'S
DIE MEISTERSINGER
VON NÜRNBERG

*which brings into your room
the beauty and grandeur of the opera*

Recorded by the full chorus of the Dresden State Opera

and

The Saxon State Orchestra, conducted by Rudolf Kempe

Starring the Metropolitan Opera Association's sensational baritone

Ferdinand Frantz...Hans Sachs

Tiana Lemnitz............Eva
Bernd Aldenhoff...........Walter von Stolzing (Bayreuth Fest. 1951)
Heinrich Pflanzl...........Beckmesser (Bayreuth Fest. 1951)
Gerhard Unger............David (Bayreuth Fest. 1951)
Kurt Böhme.............Pogner

and a company of internationally famous singers

This is a must for every music lover. A complete, uncut opera of unsurpassable artistic quality.
URLP 206   6 12" LP Records   Price: $35.70

Ask your dealer or write us for complete catalog

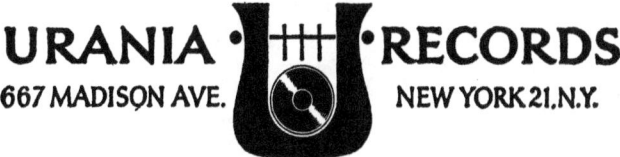

URANIA · RECORDS
667 MADISON AVE.   NEW YORK 21, N.Y.

061/20 may-7 june 1951/steinsaal des hygienemuseums/mitteldeutscher rundfunk

weber	**kempe**	lp: urania URLP 403/URLP 242-243/
der freischütz	dresden opera	URLP 5242-5243
	chorus	lp: vox OPBX 149
	trötschel	lp: acanta 22.119268
	beilke	cd: dante LYS 507-508
	aldenhoff	cd: arkadia GA 2012
	böhme	*excerpts*
	paul	lp: vox OPL 260
	faulhaber	lp: acanta 22.220281
	krämer	cd: myto MCD 961138
		cd: tahra TAH 324-327

weber	**kempe**	cd: tahra TAH 324-327
oberon;		
euryanthe		
overtures		

062/29 september 1951/sendesaal des hygienemuseums/mitteldeutscher rundfunk

bizet	**löwlein**	lp: acanta 22.223159
carmen	trötschel	
excerpt	*sung in german*	
(je dis que rien		
ne m'épouvante)		

063/15 july 1952/steinsaal des hygienemuseums/supraphon session

mendelssohn	**kempe**	78: ultraphon 23953-23957
symphony		lp: supraphon LPV 213/LPM 11-12/
no 3		E 10159/LKS 30017
"scotch"		lp: parliament PLP 142
		cd: tahra TAH 370-371

064/10-11 february 1954/steinsaal des hygienemuseums/dg sessions
mozart	**konwitschny**	lp: dg LP 16 101/LPE 17 159/2700 111/
violin	oistrakh	2726 087/478 132/89 593/89 778
concerto		lp: eterna 720 030
no 5		lp: decca (usa) DL 9766/DX 141
		lp: heliodor (usa) H 25017/HS 25017
		cd: berlin classics BC 21312
tchaikovsky		lp: dg LPE 17 163/LPM 18 196/2700 111/
violin		2726 087/2870 124/478 437/89 668
concerto		lp: eterna 820 002
		lp: decca (usa) DL 9755/DX 141
		lp: heliodor (usa) H 25071/HS 25071
		lp: supraphon DV 5410
		cd: dg 423 3992/447 4272/459 3902
		89 668 incorrectly describes orchestra as leipzig gewandhaus

065/16 february 1954/berlin jesus-christus-kirche/dg sessions
brahms	**konwitschny**	lp: dg LPM 18 199/2700 111/2726 087/
violin	oistrakh	478 137/89 607
concerto		lp: dg 820 003
		lp: decca (usa) DL 9754/DX 141
		lp: supraphon DV 5411
		cd: dg 423 3992/447 4272/459 0162/
		459 0672

066/3-4 november 1954/steinsaal des hygienemuseums/eterna sessions
beethoven	**konwitschny**	lp: eterna 820 001
symphony		lp: concertone (usa) 2002
no 3		cd: deutsche schallplatten amabile 0140 008
"eroica"		cd: berlin classics BC 90412/BC 02322
		first lp recording published by the east german eterna label; unofficial concertone issue did not name orchestra or conductor

067/1954/steinsaal des hygienemusums/eterna session
gounod	**konwitschny**	45: eterna 520 138
faust	masslennikova	
excerpt	*sung in russian*	
(ah je ris!)		

mussorgsky	**konwitschny**	lp: eterna 720 002
boris godunov	petrov	
excerpt		
(i am sick		
at heart)		

rossini	**konwitschny**	lp: eterna 720 002
il barbiere	petrov	
di siviglia	*sung in russian*	
excerpt		
(la calumnia!)		

068/5 february 1955/schauspielhaus/radio ddr
strauss	**konwitschny**	cd: pilz CD 78003/260 9342
metamorphosen		

069/may 1955/steinsaal des hygienemuseums/eterna sessions
mozart	**konwitschny**	lp: eterna 720 012
symphony		cd: berlin classics BC 93942
no 41		
"jupiter"		

beethoven		45: eterna 520 160
egmont;		
fidelio		
overtures		

070/october 1955/leipzig kongresshalle/eterna session
prokofiev	**kondrashin**	45: eterna 520 047
symphony		cd: berlin classics BC 90512
no 1		
"classical"		

070a/3 february 1956/schauspielhaus/radio ddr
mozart   **abendroth**   cd: tahra TAH 259
serenata
notturna

mozart   **abendroth**   cd: tahra TAH 259
piano concerto   askenase
no 26
"coronation"

071/14-20 june 1956/kreuzkirche/dg sessions
strauss   **konwitschny**   lp: dg LPM 18 331
sinfonia
domestica

witt   lp: dg LPE 17 077
symphony
in c "jena"

071a/10 september 1956/schauspielhaus/radio ddr
brahms   **kempe**   unpublished radio broadcast
haydn variations;
hindemith
metamorphosen;
dvorak
symphony no 9
"new world"

072/4 november 1956/schauspielhaus/radio ddr
brahms   **knappertsbusch**   cd: arkadia CD 724
symphony   cd: tahra TAH 303-304
no 3

schumann   lp: seven seas (japan) K20C 57
symphony   cd: arkadia CD 724
no 4   cd: acanta CD 74802

073/7-10 january 1957/kreuzkirche/eterna-dg sessions
mahler   **ludwig**   lp: eterna 820 028
symphony   schlemm   lp: dg LPM 18 359/478 404
no 4   cd: berlin classics BC 21192

074/february 1957/kreuzkirche/dg sessions
strauss   **böhm**   lp: dg LPM 18 378/89 644
ein heldenleben   cd: dg 423 4882/463 1902
erich mühlbach, violin soloist

075/2-3 may 1957/kreuzkirche/eterna-dg sessions
brahms	**konwitschny**	lp: eterna 820 024
piano concerto	kempff	lp: dg LPM 18 376/2548 100
no 1		cd: dg 437 3742/447 9782

076/september 1957/kreuzkirche/eterna-dg sessions
strauss	**böhm**	lp: eterna 720 041
don juan		lp: dg LPE 17 105
		cd: dg 463 1902

strauss		lp: eterna 720 041
till eulenspiegels		lp: dg LPE 17 105
lustige streiche		cd: dg 447 4542/459 3902

strauss		lp: eterna 820 062
alpensinfonie		lp: dg LPM 18 476/89 594
		cd: dg 423 4882/447 4542/463 1902

077/november 1958/kreuzkirche/eterna sessions
bach	**mauersberger**	lp: eterna 820 074-820 076
mass in	dresdner	cd: berlin classics BC 91712
b minor	kreuzchor	
	stader	
	wagner	
	haefliger	
	adam	

orchestral soloists: erich mühlbach, violin; fritz rucker, flute; kurt mahn and manfred keause, oboe d'amore; horst wiedner and wolfgang liebsche, bassoon; rudolf haase, trumpet; heinz lohan, corno di caccia; herbert collum, harpsichord and organ

078/5-13 december 1958/lukaskirche/eterna-dg sessions
strauss	**böhm**	lp: eterna 820 080-820 083
rosenkavalier	dresden opera	lp: dg LPM 18 570-18 573/
	chorus	SLPM 138 040-138 043/2711 001/
	schech	2721 162/419 1201
	seefried	cd: polygram (japan) POCG 2685-2687
	streich	*excerpts*
	francl	45: dg EPL 30 644
	böhme	lp: eterna 825 151
	fischer-dieskau	lp: dg LPM 18 656/SLPM 138 656/
		LPEM 19 410/LPEM 19 477/
		SLPEM 136 410/SLPEM 136 477/
		2535 746/2537 013/410 8471/419 3371
		cd: dg 437 6772/459 3902
		first recording in the restored lukaskirche

079/15-16 may 1959/lukaskirche/eterna sessions
shostakovich	**konwitschny**	lp: eterna 720 093-720 094
symphony		cd: berlin classics BC 90422/BC 02322
no 11
"the year 1905"

080/15-16 june 1959/lukaskirche/eterna sessions
mozart	**ancerl**	lp: eterna 820 099
symphony		lp: eurodisc NK 47304
no 36		cd: deutsche schallplatten 0140 028
"linz"		cd: berlin classics BC 90512

mozart		lp: eterna 820 099
symphony	cd: deutsche schallplatten 0140 028
no 38		cd: berlin classics BC 90512
"prague"

081/7 august 1959/kongress-saal des hygienemuseums/radio ddr
strauss	**konwitschny**	cd: pilz CD 78003/260 9342
till eulenspiegels		cd: tahra TAH 324-327
lustige streiche

082/27 november 1959/schauspielhaus/radio ddr
brahms	**knappertsbusch**	cd: tahra TAH 303-304
symphony
no 2

083/28 november 1959/schauspielhaus/radio ddr
haydn **knappertsbusch** cd: tahra TAH 303-304
symphony
no 88

strauss   cd: pilz CD 78003/260 9342
tod und   cd: arkadia CD 74802
verklärung   cd: tahra TAH 303-304

084/march 1960/lukaskirche/eterna sessions
haydn   **stein**   lp: eterna 820 196
symphonies
nos 92
"oxford"
and 103
"drum roll"

085/september 1960/lukaskirche/eterna session
mozart   **suitner**   lp: eterna 820 222/825 222/826 681
symphony   lp: philips fontana ZKY 894 041
no 29   cd: corona classics CC 00422

086/10-17 october 1960/lukaskirche/eterna-dg sessions
strauss   **böhm**   lp: eterna 820 224-225/825 224-225
elektra   borkh   lp: dg LPM 18 690-18 691/
             schech   SLPM 138 690-138 691/
             madeira   2707 011/2721 187
             uhl   cd: dg 431 7372/445 3292
             fischer-dieskau

087/november 1960/lukaskirche/eterna sessions
borodin   **sanderling** lp: eterna 820 223/825 223
symphony   lp: dg 135 139
no 2   cd: berlin classics BC 30392
                           cd: corona classics CC 01782

borodin   lp: eterna 820 223/825 223
in the steppes   lp: dg 135 011
of central asia   cd: berlin classics BC 30392/BC 93942
                           cd: edel ART 29872/43862/59722
                           cd: corona classics CC 01782

tchaikovsky   lp: eterna 820 223/825 223
romeo and   lp: dg 135 070/2538 233/2726 011
juliet   cd: berlin classics BC 30392
fantasy overture

088/november 1960/lukaskirche/eterna sessions
mozart	**suitner**	lp: eterna 820 222/825 222/826 477
eine kleine		lp: philips fontana ZKY 894 041
nachtmusik		cd: corona classics CC 00422

mozart lp: eterna 820 222/825 222/826 477
serenata cd: corona classics CC 00422
notturna

orchestral soloists: erich mühlbach and gerhard schneider, violins; alfred schindler, viola; heinz herrmann, double-bass

089/january 1961/lukaskirche/eterna sessions
haydn **kurz** lp: eterna 825 867
feldpartita
für bläser

strauss lp: eterna 825 867
wind serenade cd: berlin classics BC 93942
op 7

090/january 1961/lukaskirche/eterna session
mozart **suitner** lp: eterna 825 464
piano concerto schmidt
no 15

091/april 1961/lukaskirche/eterna sessions
mozart **suitner** lp: eterna 820 250/825 060/826 683
symphony cd: corona classics CC 00432
no 33

mozart lp: eterna 820 250/825 060
ein musikalischer cd: corona classics CC 00442
spass
erich mühlbach, violin soloist

mozart **suitner** lp: eterna 827 043
concert arias: vulpius cd: corona classics CC 009432
vorrei spiegarvi;
no che non sei
capace; non
temer amato bene

092/april 1961/lukaskirche/eterna session

verdi	**seydelmann**	lp: eterna 820 260/825 260
otello	dresden opera	
excerpts	chorus	
	friedland	
	esser	
	lauhöfer	
	sung in german	

093/may 1961/lukaskirche/eterna session

mozart	**suitner**	lp: eterna 720 156/725 021/826 715
sinfonia	tolksdorf	cd: berlin classics BC 31302
concertante	schütte	cd: corona classics CC 00972
k297b	wappler	
	schaffrath	

094/october 1961/lukaskirche/eterna-philips sessions

mozart	**suitner**	lp: eterna 820 297-299/825 297-299
entführung	dresden opera	lp: philips A02230-02231L/
aus dem	chorus	835 118-119 AY/6720 005
serail	vulpius	lp: turnabout (usa) TV 34320-34321
	rönisch	cd: berlin classics BC 91162
	apreck	*excerpts*
	förster	lp: eterna 825 116/825 304
	van mill	lp: philips GL 5670/G03098L/
		837 008 GY

095/february 1962/lukaskirche/eterna sessions

haydn	**sanderling**	lp: eterna 820 322
symphonies		lp: dg 135 034
nos 45		
"farewell"		
and 104		
"london"		

096/april 1962/lukaskirche/eterna sessions

telemann	**suitner**	lp: eterna 820 507
der schulmeister	dresdner	cd: berlin classics BC 32002
cantata	kreuzchor	
	adam	

mozart	**suitner**	lp: eterna 826 662
concert arias:	adam	
mentro ti lascio;		
per questa		
bella mano		

heinz herrmann, double-bass soloist

097/22-24 may 1962/lukaskirche/eterna sessions

mahler	**suitner**	lp: eterna 820 365/825 365
symphony		cd: berlin classics BC 30372
no 1		cd: corona classics CC 00682

debussy	45: eterna 520 471
prélude a l'apres-	lp: eterna 825 984
midi d'un faune	cd: berlin classics BC 30342

fritz rucker, flute soloist

098/may 1962/lukaskirche/eterna sessions

smetana	**suitner**	lp: eterna 820 326-328/825 326-328
the bartered	dresden opera	cd: berlin classics BC 20402
bride	chorus	*excerpts*
	schlemm	lp: eterna 720 171/820 130/820 633/
	burmeister	825 633
	lange	*recording completed in august 1962*
	apreck	
	adam	
	neukirch	
	leib	
	teschler	
	sung in german	

099/3-12 september 1962/lukaskirche/eterna sessions

stravinsky	**suitner**	lp: eterna 720 174/825 984
le sacre du		cd: berlin classics BC 30352
printemps		cd: corona classics CC 00852
tchaikovsky		lp: eterna 825 961
serenade		lp: dg 135 109/2538 232/2548 121/
for strings		2705 004/2726 011
		cd: berlin classics BC 91942

099a/26 february 1963/kongress-saal des hygienemuseums/radio ddr

shostakovich **kondrashin** unpublished radio broadcast
symphony *radio recording in conjunction with public*
no 4 *performance which was the first outside ussr*

100/august 1963/lukaskirche/eterna sessions

mozart **suitner** lp: eterna 820 464/825 464
piano concerto schmidt *weber konzertstück also recorded at these*
no 21 *sessions*

101/22-29 august 1963/lukaskirche/eterna-electrola sessions

strauss	**suitner**	lp: eterna 820 375-376/825 375-376
salome	goltz	lp: electrola E 91320-91321/STE 91320-91321
	eriksdotter	cd: berlin classics BC 91012
	melchert	*excerpts*
	hoppe	lp: eterna 820 556/825 556
	gutstein	lp: electrola E 80857/SME 80857

102/29 august-4 september 1963/lukaskirche/eterna-electrola sessions

d'albert	**schmitz**	lp: eterna 820 267-269/825 267-269
tiefland	dresden opera	lp: electrola E 91317-91319/STE 91317-91319
	chorus	cd: berlin classics BC 91082
	kuhse	*excerpts*
	rönisch	lp: eterna 820 379/825 379
	hoppe	lp: electrola E 80855/SME 80855
	gutstein	cd: berlin classics BC 20382
	adam	
	leib	

103/6 september 1963/schauspielhaus/radio ddr
eisler	**suitner**	cd: berlin classics BC 90582
ernste gesänge	leib	

103a/11 june 1964/schauspielhaus/ddr television
strauss **suitner** unpublished video recording
metamorphosen; buschner *this was a richard strauss centenary concert*
horn concerto
no 1;
also sprach
zarathustra

104/june 1964/lukaskirche/eterna session
strauss **suitner** lp: eterna 820 550/825 550
metamorphosen cd: berlin classics BC 30232

105/17-24 august 1964/lukaskirche/eterna-columbia sessions
mozart **suitner** lp: eterna 820 498-500/825 498-500
le nozze di dresden opera lp: columbia (germany) C91379-91381/
figaro chorus STC 91379-91381
  güden lp: angel SIC 6002
  rothenberger lp: emi 1C149 30159-30161/
  mathis 1C183 30159-30161
  berry cd: berlin classics BC 20962
  prey *excerpts*
  sung in german lp: eterna 820 506/825 506
    lp: columbia (germany) C 80860/SMC 80860
      SMC 80860
    lp: emi 1C063 28994
    cd: berlin classics BC 90792

106/august 1964/lukaskirche/eterna sessions
franck **sanderling** lp: eterna 820 537/825 537
symphony lp: dg 135 036/2548 132
in d minor cd: berlin classics BC 30232
  cd: corona classics CC 00942

107/2 august 1965/salzburg grosses festspielhaus/österreichischer rundfunk
bruckner **szell** cd: sony SMK 68448
symphony
no 3

108/august 1965/lukaskirche/eterna-electrola sessions

lortzing	**heger**	lp: eterna 820 597-599/825 597-599
zar und	leipzig radio	lp: electrola 1C183 29302-29304/
zimmermann	chorus	1C149 29302-29304
	köth	lp: angel SIC 6020
	burmeister	cd: emi CMS 565 7542
	schreier	*excerpts*
	gedda	lp: eterna 820 722/825 722
	prey	lp: electrola 1C063 28171/1C063 29064/
	frick	1C063 29098/1C187 29242-29243
	teschler	lp: emi HQM 1059/HQS 1059
	vogel	

109/28-29 august 1965/lukaskirche/eterna-columbia sessions

verdi	**patané**	lp: eterna 820 606/825 606
la forza del	leipzig radio	lp: columbia (germany) C 80966/
destino	chorus	SMC 80966/SHZE 361
excerpts	bumbry	lp: emi 1C063 28168
	dernesch	cd: berlin classics BC 20252
	gedda	*excerpts*
	prey	lp: emi 1C063 29064/1C137 78233-78236/
	vogel	1C063 28424/1C187 29242-29243
	frick	lp: angel 3204
	sung in german	
leoncavallo	**patané**	lp: eterna 820 650/825 650
i pagliacci	prey	lp: columbia (germany) SHZE 361
excerpt	*sung in german*	lp: emi 1C187 29242-29243
(si puo?)		

110/december 1965/lukaskirche/eterna sessions

wagenseil concerto in c for 4 harpsichords	**redel** ahlgrimm veyron-lacroix pischner ruzickova	lp: eterna 820 681/825 681 cd: berlin classics BC 31792
bach concerto for 2 harpsichords bwv 1060	**redel** ahlgrimm pischner	lp: philips 6580 089/6799 001 cd: berlin classics BC 31282
bach concerto for 2 harpsichords bwv 1061		cd: berlin classics BC 31282/BC 18662/ BC 18682
bach concerto for 2 harpsichords bwv 1062		lp: eterna 820 681/825 681 lp: philips 6580 089 cd: berlin classics BC 31282/BC 18662/ BC 18682
bach concerto for 3 harpsichords bwv 1063	**redel** ahlgrimm pischner ruzickova	cd: berlin classics BC 31792/BC 18662/ BC 18682
bach concerto for 3 harpsichords bwv 1064		lp: philips 6580 089 cd: berlin classics BC 31792/BC 18662/ BC 18682
bach concerto for 4 harpsichords bwv 1065	**redel** ahlgrimm veyron-lacroix pischner ruzickova	lp: eterna 820 681/825 681 cd: berlin classics BC 31792

111/3-6 january 1966/lukaskirche/eterna-emi sessions

strauss	**neuhaus**	lp: eterna 820 638/825 638
rosenkavalier	della casa	lp: emi ASD 2335/1C063 28518
excerpt	rothenberger	lp: angel 36436
(mir ist die ehre widerfahren)		cd: berlin classics BC 90012

strauss	lp: eterna 820 638/825 638
rosenkavalier	lp: emi ASD 2335/1C063 28518
excerpts	lp: angel 36436
(da geht er hin;	cd: berlin classics BC 90012
ist ein traum)	cd: emi CZS 567 6782

strauss	lp: eterna 820 638/825 638
arabella	cd: berlin classics BC 90012
excerpt	
(die schönen rosen/aber der richtige)	

112/may 1966/lukaskirche/eterna-philips sessions
the recordings in these sessions were completed in october 1966

schubert	**sawallisch**	lp: eterna 826 287
symphony		lp: philips SBAL 40/6729 001/6747 491
no 1		cd: philips 446 5362

schubert	lp: eterna 826 287
symphony	lp: philips SBAL 40/6729 001/6747 491
no 2	cd: philips 446 5362

schubert	lp: eterna 820 805/825 805/826 288
symphony	lp: philips SBAL 40/6729 001/6747 491
no 3	cd: philips 446 5362

schubert	lp: eterna 820 805/825 805/826 290
symphony	lp: philips SBAL 40/6539 015/6729 001/
no 4	6747 491
"tragic"	cd: philips 422 9772/446 5362

schubert	lp: eterna 820 806/825 806/826 288
symphony	lp: philips SBAL 40/SAL 3679/6527 050/
no 5	6729 001/6747 491
	cd: philips 446 5392
	cd: dg 459 3902
	also issued on lp by philips in a club edition

112/concluded
schubert   **sawallisch**   lp: eterna 820 806/825 806/826 289
symphony   lp: philips SBAL 40/SAL 3679/6729 001/
no 6   6747 491
                                          cd: philips 446 5392

schubert   lp: eterna 826 290
symphony   lp: philips SBAL 40/SAL 3672/6527 050/
no 8   6539 015/6729 001/6747 491
"unfinished"   cd: philips 422 9772/446 5392
                                          also issued on lp by philips in a club edition

schubert   lp: eterna 820 807/825 807/826 291
symphony   lp: philips SBAL 40/SAL 3702/6527 156/
no 9   6570 054/6580 207/6729 001/
"great"   6747 491
                                          cd: philips 446 5392
                                          also issued on lp by philips in a club edition

schubert   lp: eterna 826 289
overture in c   lp: philips SBAL 40/SAL 3672/6729 001/
in the italian   6747 491
style   cd: philips 446 5362

schubert   lp: eterna 826 289
overture in d   lp: philips SBAL 40/SAL 3672/6729 001/
in the italian   6747 491
style   cd: philips 446 5362

113/1966/lukaskirche/eterna sessions

handel   **kurz**   lp: eterna 820 711/825 711
ariodante   schreier   cd: berlin classics BC 91392/BC 91412
excerpt
(es breiten sich
die schwingen
der liebe);
strauss
capriccio excerpt
(kein andres das
mir so im herzen);
lortzing
undine excerpt
(vater, mutter!)

nicolai   lp: eterna 820 711/825 711
die lustigen weiber
von windsor
excerpt
(horch die lerche!);
lortzing
zar und zimmermann
excerpt
(leb wohl mein
flandrisch mädchen!)

bizet   **kurz**   lp: eterna 820 711/825 711
carmen excerpt   schreier
(la fleur que   *sung in german*
tu m'avais jetée);
verdi
la traviata excerpt
(deh miei bollenti);
boieldieu
la dame blanche
excerpt
(viens gentille dame!);
massenet
manon excerpts
(en fermant les yeux;
ah fuyez douce image!);
tchaikovsky
evgeny onegin excerpt
(faint echo of my youth)

114/october 1966/lukaskirche/eterna-dg session

henze	**henze**	lp: eterna 820 709/825 709
musen	dresdner	lp: dg 139 374
siziliens	kreuzchor	cd: dg 449 8602/449 8702
	moser	
	rollino and	
	sheftel, pianos	

115/23-25 october 1966/lukaskirche/eterna-emi sessions

mozart **suitner** lp: eterna 820 739/825 739
zauberflöte prey lp: emi 1C063 29087
excerpts cd: berlin classics BC 31492
(der vogelfänger *items marked with an asterisk also re-issued*
bin ich ja!*; *on emi cd CDM 769 5072*
ein mädchen oder
weibchen;
papagena, papageno!);
cosi fan tutte
excerpts
(rivolgete a lui
lo sguardo; donne
mie la fate e tanti);
don giovanni
excerpts
(fin ch'an dal vino;
deh vieni alla finestra;
meta di voi qua vadamo;
ho capito signore!);
le nozze di figaro
excerpts
(se vuol ballare;
non piu andrai;
aprite un po quel occhi;
hai gia vinta la
causa!*)

116/february 1967/lukaskirche/eterna sessions

weber	**sanderling**	lp: eterna 820 690/825 690
clarinet	michallik	cd: berlin classics BC 30222/BC 93942
concerto		cd: corona classics CC 00612
no 1		cd: philips 462 8682

weber	lp: eterna 820 690/825 690
clarinet	cd: berlin classics BC 30222
concerto	cd: corona classics CC 00612
no 2	cd: philips 462 8682

117/28 february 1967/lukaskirche/eterna session

hindemith	**suitner**	lp: eterna 825 843
symphonic		cd: berlin classics BC 30412/BC 93942
metamorphoses		
on themes		
of weber		

118/27-29 august 1967/lukaskirche/eterna sessions

mozart	**suitner**	lp: eterna 820 772/825 772
entführung	schreier	*wie stark ist nicht dein zauberton also on*
aus dem serail		*eurodisc lp 302 203.420*
excerpts		
(hier soll ich dich		
denn sehen?;		
wenn der freude;		
ich baue ganz);		
zauberflöte		
excerpt		
(wie stark ist nicht		
dein zauberton);		
cosi fan tutte		
excerpt		
(tradito schernito!);		
don giovanni		
excerpt		
(il mio tesoro);		
la clemenza di tito		
excerpt		
(se all'impero!)		

mozart	**suitner**	lp: eterna 820 772/825 772
entführung	schreier	cd: berlin classics BC 91392/BC 91412
aus dem serail		*dies bildnis also on eurodisc lp 302 203.420*
excerpt		
(konstanze dich		
wiederzusehen?);		
zauberflöte		
excerpt		
(dies bildnis);		
cosi fan tutte		
excerpt		
(un aura amorosa);		
don giovanni		
excerpt		
(dalla sua pace)		

volkmann	**suitner**	lp: eterna 825 961
serenade for		cd: berlin classics BC 91942
strings		
no 2		

119/6-13 november 1967/lukaskirche/eterna-philips sessions

haydn	**jochum**	lp: eterna 826 006
symphony		cd: berlin classics BC 90342
no 93		

haydn lp: eterna 826 006
symphony cd: berlin classics BC 90342
no 94
"surprise"

haydn lp: eterna 826 031
symphony lp: philips 6530 066
no 95 cd: berlin classics BC 90342/BC 93942

haydn lp: eterna 826 031
symphony lp: philips 6530 066
no 98 cd: berlin classics BC 90342

120/1967/kongressaal des hygienemuseums/radio ddr
kurz **kurz** lp: eterna 820 938
piano kootz
concerto

121/1967/lukaskirche/eterna session
kurzbach **kurz** lp: eterna 885 072
concertino mitzscherling
for piano
and strings

121a/11-12 january 1968/schauspielhaus/radio ddr
bruckner   **kempe**   unpublished radio broadcast
symphony   *recording survives in mono version only*
no 8

122/april-may 1968/lukaskirche/eterna sessions
mozart   **suitner**   lp: eterna 826 682
symphony   cd: ars vivendi 2100 108/MRC 008
no 31
"paris"

mozart   lp: eterna 826 102
symphony   cd: ars vivendi 2100 107/MRC 007
no 35
"haffner"

mozart   lp: eterna 826 102
symphony   cd: ars vivendi 2100 107/MRC 007
no 36
"linz"

mozart   lp: eterna 826 465
symphony   cd: ars vivendi 2100 108/MRC 008
no 38
"prague"

123/26 june-6 july 1968/lukaskirche/eterna-emi sessions
strauss   **kempe**   lp: eterna 826 009-826 011
ariadne   janowitz   lp: emi SAN 215-217/SLS 936/
auf naxos   geszty   1C163 00110-00112/2C165 00110-00112
                  zylis-gara   lp: angel 3733
                  king   cd: emi CMS 764 1592
                  prey   *excerpts*
                  adam   lp: emi 1C063 00824/100 8241

124/august 1968/lukaskirche/eterna session
reger   **bongartz**   lp: eterna 826 063
variations   cd: berlin classics BC 21772/BC 93942
and fugue
on a theme
of mozart

125/6-10 january 1969/lukaskirche/eterna sessions

strauss	**suitner**	lp: eterna 826 097
rosenkavalier	dresden opera	lp: telefunken SAT 22513
excerpt	chorus	cd: berlin classics BC 92152
(da lieg' ich);	schröter	
die frau ohne	adam	
schatten		
(sie aus dem		
hause!/sie haben		
es mir gesagt)		
strauss	**suitner**	lp: eterna 826 097
daphne excerpt	schröter	lp: telefunken SAT 22513
(seid ihr um	adam	cd: berlin classics BC 92152
mich, ihr		
hirten alle?)		
strauss	**suitner**	lp: eterna 826 097
die schweigsame	adam	lp: telefunken SAT 22513
frau excerpt		cd: berlin classics BC 91212/BC 92152/
(wie schön ist		BC 93942
doch die musik)		
strauss		lp: eterna 826 097
capriccio excerpt		lp: telefunken SAT 22513
(hola ihr streiter		cd: berlin classics BC 91212/BC 92152
in apoll!)		

126/19-27 march 1969/lukaskirche/eterna-dg sessions

beethoven	**böhm**	lp: eterna 826 055-826 057
fidelio	leipzig radio	lp: dg 2709 031/2720 113/2721 136
	chorus	cd: dg 445 6752/447 9252
	jones	*excerpts*
	mathis	lp: eterna 826 058
	king	lp: dg 2530 958/2535 135/2537 002
	schreier	cd: dg 413 1452/427 1942/
	adam	437 9282/459 3902
	crass	*this recording included leonore no 3 overture*
	talvela	*which was placed on a separate lp side*

127/august 1969/lukaskirche/eterna session

suppé	**suitner**	lp: eterna 845 053
schöne galathea;		lp: philips 6580 113
poet and		cd: berlin classics BC 21532
peasant;		
light cavalry;		
pique dame;		
morning noon and		
night in vienna;		
jolly robbers;		
flotte burschen		
overtures		

128/9-13 november 1969/lukaskirche/eterna sessions

humperdinck	**suitner**	lp: eterna 826 177-826 178
hänsel und	leipzig radio	lp: telefunken 635.074 DX
gretel	chorus	cd: telefunken 835 074 ZA
	hoff	cd: berlin classics BC 0220 007
	springer	*excerpts*
	krahmer	lp: eterna 826 179
	schröter	
	schreier	
	adam	

128/concluded
mozart　　　　　**suitner**　　　lp: eterna 825 662
le nozze di　　　adam
figaro excerpts
(se vuol ballare;
non piu andrai;
aprite un po;
hai gia vinta la causa);
don giovanni
excerpts
(madamina; fin
ch'han dal vino;
ah pieta signori miei;
deh vieni alla finestra;
meta di voi);
die zauberflöte
excerpts
(der vogelfänger
bin ich ja; ein
mädchen oder weibchen);
zaide excerpts
(wer hungrig bei
der tafel sitzt; ihr
mächtigen seht
ungerührt);
concert aria: männer
suchen stets zu naschen

129/1969/lukaskirche/eterna session
hohensee   **kegel**   lp: eterna 825 920
hier bin ich
mensch
film symphony
in 5 movements

130/march 1970/lukaskirche/eterna sessions
mussorgsky   **kegel**   lp: eterna 825 970
boris   leipzig radio   lp: telefunken 641.290 AS
godunov   chorus   cd: berlin classics BC 20322
excerpts   kuhse
   schreier
   ritzmann
   hölzke
   adam
   vogel
   sung in german

131/march 1970/lukaskirche/eterna sessions
lanner   **suitner**   lp: eterna 845 081
hofballtänze;
steyrische tänze;
schönbrunner
waltzes

josef strauss   lp: eterna 845 081
pizzicato polka;
auf ferienreisen;
frauenherz;
moulinet;
die libelle;
feuerfest;
plappermäulchen
polkas

132/march-april 1970/lukaskirche/eterna sessions

strauss horn concerti nos 1 and 2	**rögner** damm	lp: eterna 825 883 lp: eurodisc PK 80736 cd: berlin classics BC 91802

butting piano concerto	**rögner** ander	lp: eterna 825 890 *another work by this east german composer was scheduled for recording by eterna and was even allocated a catalogue number (720 173), but no evidence can be found that this actually took place*

finke capriccio on a polish folk song for piano and orchestra	**rögner** schorler	lp: eterna 825 890/885 074

133/24-27 april 1970/lukaskirche/eterna sessions

mozart concert arias: a berenice sol nascente; non curo l'affeto; fra cento affanni voi avete un cor fedele; ma che vi fece o stelle!; sperai vivino il lido; mia speranza adorata; ah non sai qual pensa sia il doverti; no che non sai capace	**suitner** geszty	lp: eterna 825 729

134/april 1970/lukaskirche/eterna session
wagner   **müller-sybel**   eterna unpublished
meistersinger   dresden opera
von nürnberg   chorus
excerpt
(wach auf!)

135/18-23 may 1970/lukaskirche/eterna-philips sessions
vivaldi   **negri**   lp: eterna 825 955
concerto per   lp: philips 6500 242/6768 013/6797 001
dresda;
concerto in c

vivaldi   lp: eterna 825 955
concerto in c;   lp: philips 6500 242/6768 013
concerto in g minor
soloists: arndt schöne and wilfried gärtner, flutes; manfred weise and hans tuppak, salmo; kurt mahn, oboe; wolfgang liebscher, bassoon; peter mirring, reinhard ulbricht, joachim bischof, alfred schindler, joachim zindler, friedrich franke and arthur meyer, violins; erhard and elisabeth vietz, mandolins; roland zimmer and franz just, lutes; clemens dillner, cello; hans otto, harpsichord; christoph albrecht, organ

136/13-24 june 1970/lukaskirche/eterna-emi sessions
strauss   **kempe**   lp: eterna 826 438
don juan   lp: emi SLS 861/1C197 50271-50274/
                                       ED 29 00531/1C063 02342
                                lp: angel 60288
                                cd: emi CDC 747 8652/CMS 764 3422/
                                       CZS 568 1102/CZS 573 6142/
                                       CDE 574 5902

strauss   lp: eterna 826 437
till eulenspiegels   lp: emi SLS 894/1C195 52100-52102/
lustige streiche   ESD 7026/ED 29 00531/1C063 02344
                                lp: angel 60279
                                cd: emi CDC 747 8622/CMS 764 3422/
                                     CZS 568 1102/CZS 573 6142/
                                     CDE 574 5902

strauss   eterna-emi unpublished
intermezzo
act 2 entr'acte

136/concluded

strauss
tod und
verklärung
	kempe	lp: eterna 826 437
		lp: emi SLS 880/1C195 50344-50346/
		    ED 29 00531/1C063 02344
		lp: angel 60279
		cd: emi CDC 747 8622/CMS 764 3462/
		    CZS 568 1102/CZS 573 6142

strauss   lp: eterna 826 439
capriccio
excerpt
(mondscheinmusik)
peter damm, horn solo

strauss   lp: eterna 826 439
der bürger als   lp: emi SLS 861/1C195 50271-50274
edelmann   cd: emi CMS 764 3462/CZS 573 6142
peter mirring, violin solo; clemens dillner, cello solo; rudolf haase, trumpet solo; walter olbertz, piano solo ; kurt mahn, oboe solo

strauss   lp: eterna 826 437
salome   lp: emi SLS 894/1C195 52100-52102/
excerpt   ESD 7026/ED 29 00531/1C063 02344
(dance of the   lp: angel 60297
7 veils)   cd: emi CDC 747 3462/CMS 764 3462/
                                                CZS 573 6142/CDE 574 5902

137/15 june 1970/lukaskirche/eterna rehearsal tapes
beethoven	**kempe**	lp: eterna 827 201
symphony		lp: orfeo S079 832I
no 7		cd: berlin classics BC 91952/BC 93942

beethoven		lp: eterna 827 201
egmont		lp: orfeo S079 832I
overture		cd: berlin classics BC 91952
		also announced for publication by berlin classics in dvd audio format

138/27 june-4 july 1970/lukaskirche/eterna sessions
mozart	**suitner**	lp: eterna 826 173-826 175
zauberflöte	leipzig radio	lp: eurodisc XGR 80584
	chorus	cd: rca/bmg 74321 322402
	donath	*excerpts*
	geszty	lp: eterna 826 176
	hoff	lp: eurodisc 302 203.420
	schreier	
	leib	
	adam	
	vogel	

139/august 1970/lukaskirche/eterna sessions
rosenfeld	**bauer**	lp: eterna 885 105
piano	rösel	
concerto		

rosenfeld	**bauer**	lp: eterna 885 105
cello	schwab	
concerto		

140/24 november-1 december 1970/lukaskirche/eterna-emi sessions
wagner	**karajan**	lp: eterna 826 227-826 231
meistersinger	dresden opera	lp: emi SLS 957/EX 749 6831/
von nürnberg	chorus	1C157 02174-02178/1C193 02174-02178/
	leipzig radio	2C165 02174-02178/3C165 02174-02178
	chorus	lp: angel 3776
	donath	cd: emi CDS 749 6832/CMS 567 0862
	hesse	*excerpts*
	kollo	lp: eterna 826 192/826 265
	schreier	lp: emi SEOM 18/1C063 02233/
	adam	1C047 02381
	ridderbusch	cd: emi CDM 763 4522/CDM 769 3382/
	evans	CZS 252 1592

recording session for die zauberflöte: otmar suitner and helen donath (seated) and peter schreier (extreme right)

141/february 1971/lukaskirche/eterna sessions

weber	**rögner**	lp: eterna 826 131
abu hassan	leipzig radio	lp: eurodisc MR 80680
	chorus	cd: rca/bmg 74321 405772
	hallstein	*excerpts*
	schreier	lp: eurodisc 302 203.420
	adam	

britten	**kegel**	lp: eterna 826 305
variations and		lp: eurodisc XBK 89518
fugue on a		cd: nova 970032
theme of		
purcell		

142/22-29 may 1971/lukaskirche/eterna-emi sessions

mozart	**schmidt-**	lp: eterna 826 261-826 264
idomeneo	**isserstedt**	lp: emi SLS 965/1C191 29271-29274/
	leipzig radio	2C169 29271-29274/3C165 29271-29274
	chorus	cd: emi CMS 763 9902
	rothenberger	*excerpts*
	moser	lp: eterna 826 292
	gedda	lp: emi 1C063 28965
	schreier	
	dallapozza	
	adam	

143/june 1971/lukaskirche/eterna-philips sessions

schubert	**sawallisch**	lp: eterna 826 216
mass no 5	leipzig radio	lp: philips 6500 329
d678	chorus	cd: philips 426 6542
	donath	
	springer	
	schreier	
	adam	

schubert	**sawallisch**	lp: eterna 826 215
mass no 6	leipzig radio	lp: philips 6500 330/416 8621
d950	chorus	cd: philips 426 6542
	donath	
	springer	
	schreier	
	rotzsch	
	adam	

144/june 1971/lukaskirche/eterna session
prokofiev **kegel** lp: eterna 826 305
peter and r.ludwig lp: eurodisc XBK 89518/201 991.250
the wolf cd: nova 970032

145/august 1971/steinsaal des hygienemuseums/soundtrack recording for italian television (rai) film
verdi **molinari-** lp: acanta HA 21472
rigoletto **pradelli** cd: acanta 44.41472
    dresden opera cd: austrophon 870 1582
    chorus *also published on laserdisc in japan*
    rinaldi
    cortez
    bonisolli
    panerai
    rundgren

146/5-15 september 1971/lukaskirche/eterna-emi sessions
strauss **kempe** lp: eterna 826 438
also sprach lp: emi SLS 861/1C191 50271-50274/
zarathustra   ESD 7026/ED 29 08011/1C063 02342
christian funke, violin solo lp: angel 60283
  cd: emi CDC 747 8622/CMS 764 3462/
    CZS 568 1102/CZS 573 6142/
    CDE 574 5902
  dvd audio: emi DVC 492 3969

strauss lp: eterna 826 625
ein heldenleben lp: emi SLS 880/1C195 50344-50346
peter mirring, violin solo lp: angel 60315
  cd: emi CMS 764 3422/CDM 769 1712/
    CZS 568 1102/CZS 573 6142

strauss lp: eterna 826 439
schlagobers lp: emi SLS 861/1C191 50271-50274
waltz cd: emi CMS 764 3462/CZS 573 6142

strauss lp: eterna 826 440
alpensinfonie lp: emi SLS 861/1C191 50271-50274/
    ASD 3173/1C063 02341
  cd: emi CMS 764 3502/CZS 573 6142
  dvd audio: emi DVC 492 3969

147/4-12 october 1971/lukaskirche/eterna-emi sessions

donizetti	**kurz**	lp: eterna 826 277
don pasquale	leipzig radio	lp: emi 1C063 29055
excerpts	chorus	cd: berlin classics BC 20312
	rothenberger	
	schreier	
	süss	
	leib	
	sung in german	

verdi	**kurz**	lp: eterna 826 297
rigoletto	leipzig radio	lp: emi 1C063 29056
excerpts	chorus	cd: berlin classics BC 20282
	rothenberger	
	burmeister	
	ilosfalvy	
	wixell	
	sung in german	

verdi	**patané**	lp: eterna 826 298
la traviata	leipzig radio	lp: emi 1C063 29054
excerpts	chorus	cd: berlin classics BC 20272
	rothenberger	
	de ridder	
	anheisser	
	sung in german	

148/3-6 november 1971/lukaskirche/eterna sessions

brahms	**sanderling**	lp: eterna 826 314
symphony		lp: eurodisc XFK 27945
no 1		lp: victor SB 6873/GL 32561
		cd: rca/bmg 74321 212852/74321 303672

149/december 1971/lukaskirche/eterna sessions
j.strauss **garaguly** lp: eterna 845 099
wiener blut cd: berlin classics BC 92192
overture;
auf der jagd;
kaiserwalzer;
im krapfenwald'l;
ägytischer marsch;
morgenblätter;
tritsch-tratsch
polka; perpetuum
mobile; rosen
aus dem süden

150/22-23 april 1971/kulturpalast/ddr television
tchaikovsky **siepuch** unpublished video recording
violin oistrakh *david oistrakh's final appearance in german*
concerto *democratic republic*

151/10-13 january 1972/lukaskirche/eterna sessions
brahms **sanderling** lp: eterna 826 315
symphony lp: victor SB 6875/GL 32562
no 2 cd: rca/bmg 74321 178942/74321 303672

152/12 february 1972/lukaskirche/eterna sessions

mozart   **suitner**   lp: eterna 826 334
entführung   schreier   cd: berlin classics BC 20432
aus dem serail   adam
excerpt   *french, italian*
(vivat bacchus!);   *and czech items*
zauberflöte   *sung in german*
excerpts
(die wahrheitslehre
dieser knaben;
bewahret euch vor
weibertücken;
pamina wo bist du?);
lortzing
undine
excerpts
(in wein ist
wahrheit; o wie
köstlich ist das
reisen);
bizet
les pecheurs de
perles
excerpt
(au fond du
temple saint);
smetana
bartered bride
excerpt
(komm mein
söhnchen);
verdi
la forza del
destino
excerpt
(solenne in
quest' ora);
gounod
faust
excerpt
(me voici! d'ou
vient ta surprise?)

153/8-13 march 1972/lukaskirche/eterna sessions
brahms	**sanderling**	lp: eterna 826 317
symphony		lp: victor SB 6879
no 4		cd: rca/bmg 74321 242062/74321 303672

brahms	lp: eterna 826 317
tragic	lp: victor SB 6875/GL 32562
overture	cd: rca/bmg 74321 212852/74321 303672/ 74321 845882

154/26-30 march 1972/lukaskirche/eterna-emi sessions
strauss	**kempe**	lp: eterna 826 441
sinfonia		lp: emi SLS 894/1C195 52100-52102
domestica		cd: emi CMS 764 3462/CZS 573 6142

155/april 1972/lukaskirche/eterna sessions
bizet	**suitner**	lp: eterna 826 342
symphony		cd: berlin classics BC 90402/BC 93942
in c		

weber	lp: eterna 826 342
symphony	cd: berlin classics BC 90402
in c	

156/may 1972/lukaskirche/eterna-philips sessions
leclair	**negri**	lp: eterna 826 350
oboe concerto	holliger	lp: philips 6500 413
in c;		
marcello		
oboe concerto		
in d minor;		
vivaldi		
oboe concerto		
in d minor;		
telemann		
oboe d'amore		
concerto in g		

157/6-11 june 1972/lukaskirche/eterna sessions
brahms	**sanderling**	lp: eterna 826 316
symphony		lp: victor SB 6877/GL 32563
no 3		cd: rca/bmg 74321 178942/74321 303672

brahms	lp: eterna 826 316
haydn	lp: victor SB 6877/GL 32563
variations	cd: rca/bmg 74321 242 062/74321 303672

158/23-25 june 1972/lukaskirche/dg sessions
brahms	**abbado**	lp: dg 2530 452/2535 293/2720 061
symphony		cd: belart 461 0842
no 3		

brahms	lp: dg 2530 452/2535 293
haydn	cd: belart 461 0842
variations	

159/13 august 1972/salzburg grosses festspielhaus/österreichischer rundfunk
bartok	**karajan**	cd: dg 447 6662
piano concerto	anda	cd: as-disc NAS 2508
no 3		

schumann	**karajan**	cd: dg 447 6662
symphony		
no 4		

160/15 august 1972/salzburg grosses festspielhaus/österreichischer rundfunk
strauss	**böhm**	cd: dg 423 4882/463 1902
tod und		
verklärung		

161/1-12 september 1972/lukaskirche/eterna-emi sessions

schumann   sawallisch   lp: eterna 826 906
symphony   lp: emi SLS 867/SXLP 30526/
no 1   1C063 02418/1C149 02418-02420/
"spring"   1C183 02418-02420
                                              cd: emi CDM 769 4712/CMS 764 8152

schumann   lp: eterna 826 907
symphony   lp: emi SLS 867/1C149 02418-02420/
no 2   1C183 02418-02420
                                              cd: emi CMS 764 8152/CDM 769 4722

schumann   lp: eterna 826 908
symphony   lp: emi SLS 867/1C149 02418-02420/
no 3   1C183 02418-02420
"rhenish"   cd: emi CMS 764 8152/CDM 769 4722

schumann   lp: eterna 826 906
symphony   lp: emi SLS 867/SXLP 30526/
no 4   1C063 02418/1C149 02418-02420/
                                              1C183 02418-02420
                                              cd: emi CDM 769 4712/CMS 764 8152

schumann   lp: eterna 826 907
overture   lp: emi SLS 867/1C149 02418-02420/
scherzo and   1C183 02418-02420
finale   cd: emi CDM 769 4712/CDZ 568 0632

schumann   lp: eterna 826 908
manfred   lp: emi SLS 867/1C149 02418-02420/
overture   1C183 02418-02420

162/13-20 october 1972/lukaskirche/eterna-emi sessions

bizet	**patané**	lp: eterna 826 373
carmen	leipzig radio	lp: emi 1C063 29091
excerpts	chorus	cd: berlin classics BC 20302
	dresden	
	philharmonic	
	childrens'	
	chorus	
	fassbänder	
	rothenberger	
	spiess	
	anheisser	
	sung in german	
verdi	**patané**	lp: eterna 826 436
aida	leipzig radio	lp: emi 1C063 29090
excerpts	chorus	cd: berlin classics BC 20262
	bjoner	
	schröter	
	spiess	
	vogel	
	stryczek	
	sung in german	
puccini	**patané**	lp: eterna 826 435
turandot	leipzig radio	lp: emi 1C063 29092
excerpts	chorus	cd: berlin classics BC 20292
	dresden	
	philharmonic	
	childrens'	
	chorus	
	bjoner	
	rothenberger	
	spiess	
	vogel	
	sung in german	

163/november-december 1972/lukaskirche/eterna-philips sessions

vivaldi	**negri**	lp: eterna 826 393-826 394
concerti for	giuranna	lp: philips 6768 013
viola d'amore		
and orchestra		

orchestral soloists: kurt mahn and manfred krause, oboes; günter angerhöfer, bassoon; peter damm and siegfried gizyki, horns; gerhard pluswik, cello; bernd haubold, violin; roland zimmer, lute; christiane jaccottet, harpsichord

mozart	**de waart**	lp: eterna 826 573
serenade		lp: philips 6500 627/6747 378/6770 043
no 9		
"posthorn";		
2 marches		
in d k335		

164/28 december 1972-5 january 1973/lukaskirche/eterna sessions

j.strauss	**kempe**	lp: eterna 845 105
g'schichten		lp: eurodisc 86847 IU
aus dem		lp: victor LRL1-5044
wienerwald		cd: berlin classics BC 90072/BC 90752

j.strauss	lp: eterna 845 105
die fledermaus	lp: eurodisc 86847 IU
overture	lp: victor LRL1-5044
	cd: berlin classics BC 90072/BC 93942

josef strauss	lp: eterna 845 105
sphärenklänge	lp: eurodisc 86847 IU
waltz	lp: victor LRL1-5044
	cd: berlin classics BC 90072/BC 93942

suppé	lp: eterna 845 105
morning noon	lp: eurodisc 86847 IU
and night in	lp: victor LRL1-5044
vienna	cd: berlin classics BC 90072/BC 90752
overture	

clemens dillner, cello soloist

164/concluded
lehar **kempe** lp: eterna 845 105
gold und lp: eurodisc 86847 IU
silber lp: victor LRL1-5044
waltz cd: berlin classics BC 90072/BC 90752

j.strauss lp: eterna 845 105
leichtes blut lp: eurodisc 86847 IU
polka lp: victor LRL1-5044
cd: berlin classics BC 90072

165/1-5 january 1973/lukaskirche/eterna-emi sessions
strauss **kempe** lp: eterna 826 626
macbeth lp: emi SLS 861/1C191 50271-50274
lp: angel 60288
cd: emi CMS 764 3502/CDM 769 1712/
CZS 573 6142

strauss lp: eterna 826 626
metamorphosen lp: emi SLS 861/1C191 50271-50274
cd: emi CMS 764 3502/CZS 573 6142

166/28 january-8 february 1973/lukaskirche/eterna-dg sessions
weber **kleiber** lp: eterna 826 431-826 433
der freischütz leipzig radio lp: dg 2709 046
chorus cd: dg 415 4322/457 7362
janowitz *excerpts*
mathis lp: eterna 826 430
schreier lp: dg 2537 020
adam cd: dg 439 4402/459 3902
weikl
vogel
crass

clemens dillner, cello soloist; joachim ulbricht, viola soloist

167/february 1973/lukaskirche/eterna sessions
recordings in these sessions were completed in april 1973

mozart flute concerti nos 1 and 2; andante in c for flute and orchestra	**blomstedt** walter	lp: eterna 826 559 cd: berlin classics BC 30262
mozart oboe concerto in c	**blomstedt** mahn	lp: eterna 826 559 cd: ars vivendi 2100 215

168/5-6 march 1973/lukaskirche/eterna sessions

mozart symphony no 41 "jupiter"	**suitner**	lp: eterna 826 465 cd: corona classics CC 00422
mozart notturno k286; serenade in f k101		lp: eterna 826 477 cd: corona classics CC 00442

169/22-29 june 1973/lukaskirche/eterna-emi sessions

strauss don quixote	**kempe** tortelier rostal	lp: eterna 826 624 lp: emi SLS 880/ASD 3074/ED 29 08011/ 1C195 50344-50346 lp: angel 37046 cd: emi CDC 747 8652/CZS 573 6142
strauss dance suite on themes of couperin	**kempe**	lp: eterna 826 627 lp: emi SLS 880/1C195 50344-50346 cd: emi CMS 764 3402/CZS 573 6142/ CMS 764 3502

strauss
rosenkavalier
waltzes
		lp: eterna 826 624
		lp: emi SLS 880/ASD 3074/
		    1C195 50344-50346
		lp: angel 37046
		cd: emi CZS 568 1102/CZS 573 6142/
		    CMS 764 3462

170/june 1973/lukaskirche/eterna-philips sessions

vivaldi	**negri**	lp: eterna 826 495
violin concerti	grumiaux	lp: philips 6500 690
in e flat,		cd: philips 423 2812
e minor,		
a minor and		
g minor		

171/5-7 july 1973/lukaskirche/eterna sessions

brahms	**rögner**	lp: eterna 826 560
hungarian		lp: eurodisc 201.986 250
dances;		
academic		
festival overture		
handel	**rögner**	lp: eterna 826 554
harp concerto	zoff	cd: berlin classics BC 93942
in b flat		cd: ars vivendi 2100 167
dittersdorf		lp: eterna 826 554
harp concerto		cd: ars vivendi 2100 167
in a flat		
francaix		lp: eterna 826 554
jeux poétiques		cd: ars vivendi 2100 167
pour harpe et		
orchestre		

172/5-12 september 1973/lukaskirche/eterna-dg sessions

mozart	**böhm**	lp: eterna 826 512-826 514
entführung	leipzig radio	lp: dg 2709 051/2740 102/2740 203/
aus dem	chorus	2740 222
serail	auger	cd: dg 423 4592/429 8682/435 3952
	grist	*excerpts*
	schreier	lp: eterna 826 521
	neukirch	lp: dg 2535 229/2535 627/2537 035/
	moll	2563 649/2721 205
		cd: dg 413 1812/459 3902

orchestral soloists: peter mirring, violin; clemens dillner, cello; johannes walter, flute; wolfgang holzhäuser, oboe

mozart	**böhm**	lp: eterna 826 512-826 514
der schauspiel-	auger	lp: dg 2709 051/2740 102/2740 203/
direktor	grist	2740 222
	schreier	cd: dg 419 5662/429 8772/435 3952
	moll	*excerpts*
		lp: dg 2535 229

173/4 october 1973/kulturpalast/radio ddr

weber	**blomstedt**	cd: pilz AS 20582
euryanthe		
overture;		
mozart		
symphony		
no 38		
"prague"		

beethoven	cd: pilz AS 20592
symphony	
no 3	
"eroica"	

174/17-23 november 1973/lukaskirche/eterna-philips sessions

mozart	**de waart**	lp: eterna 826 572
serenade	ughi	lp: philips 6500 696/6747 378/6770 043
no 7		
"haffner"		

mozart   **de waart**   lp: eterna 826 572
march in d   lp: philips 6500 696/6747 378/6770 043
k249

mozart   lp: eterna 826 570
serenade   lp: philips 6500 695/6747 378
no 4
k203

march   lp: eterna 826 570
in d   lp: philips 6500 695/6747 378
k237

serenade   lp: eterna 826 571
no 5   lp: philips 6500 697/6747 378
k204

march   lp: eterna 826 571
in d   lp: philips 6500 697/6747 378
k215

175/2-7 january 1974/lukaskirche/eterna sessions
recordings in these sessions were completed in october 1974

mozart symphony no 28	**suitner**	lp: eterna 826 681
mozart symphony no 30		lp: eterna 826 682
mozart symphony no 32		lp: eterna 826 683
mozart symphony no 34		lp: eterna 826 683 cd: berlin classics BC 93942

176/march 1974/lukaskirche/eterna-emi sessions

strauss   **kempe**   lp: eterna 826 628
aus italien   lp: emi SLS 894/1C195 52100-52102/
                                    1C063 02523
                               lp: angel 60301
                               cd: emi CMS 764 3502/CZS 573 6142

strauss   lp: eterna 826 627
josephslegende   lp: emi SLS 894/1C195 52100-52102
symphonic   cd: emi CMS 764 3462/CZS 573 6142
fragment

177/march-april 1974/lukaskirche/eterna sessions

mozart   **blomstedt**   lp: eterna 826 680
horn concerti   damm   lp: eurodisc KK 88303
nos 1, 2, 3   cd: rca/bmg VD 69254/74321 405082
and 4;
rondo k371
for horn and
orchestra

Staatskapelle Dresden

Donnerstag, 14. März 1974
Freitag, 15. März 1974
20 Uhr, Kulturpalast

8. Sinfoniekonzert

Gastdirigent
Rudolf Kempe
Solist
Malcolm Frager, Klavier

Claude Debussy (1862–1918)
Prélude à l'Après-midi d'un faune
(Vorspiel zum Nachmittag eines Faun)

Robert Schumann (1810–1856)
Konzert für Klavier und Orchester a-Moll, op. 54
Allegro affettuoso
Intermezzo. Andantino grazioso
Allegro vivace

Pause

Richard Strauss (1864–1949)
Ein Heldenleben, op. 40
Tondichtung für großes Orchester

Öffentliche Generalprobe
14. März 1974, 11 Uhr

Das Konzert am 15. März 1974
wird von Radio DDR, Sender Dresden,
im Rahmen der „Dresdner Abende"
original übertragen

178/25 april 1974/kulturpalast/radio ddr
kunad kurz cd: private issue HT 5307
quadrophonie
für 4 streich-
orchester,
blechbläser und
pauken

179/5-6 may 1974/lukaskirche/eterna session
dvorak blomstedt lp: eterna 826 763
symphony cd: berlin classics BC 90242/BC 93942
no 8

180/26 june-8 july 1974/lukaskirche/eterna-emi sessions
weber janowski lp: eterna 826 716-826 718
euryanthe leipzig radio lp: emi SLS 983/1C191 02591-02594
  chorus cd: emi CMS 763 5092
  norman cd: berlin classics BC 11082
  hunter *excerpts*
  gedda lp: eterna 826 829
  krause cd: berlin classics BC 30222/BC 93942
  vogel

181/26 august-5 september 1974/lukaskirche/eterna-emi sessions
wagner hollreiser lp: eterna 826 658-826 662
rienzi leipzig radio lp: emi SLS 990/1C193 02776-02780
  chorus cd: emi CMS 763 9802
  dresden opera *excerpts*
  chorus lp: eterna 826 663
  wennberg lp: emi 1C061 03489
  kollo *janis martin replaced brigitte fassbänder;*
  schreier *recording completed in february and april 1976*
  hillebrand
  adam
  vogel

182/october 1974/lukaskirche/eterna sessions
matthus **blomstedt** lp: eterna 885 105
piano schmidt cd: berlin classics BC 93942
concerto

183/21-22 november 1974/lukaskirche/eterna session
mozart **suitner** lp: eterna 826 852
symphony
no 39

184/november 1974/lukaskirche/eterna sessions
kurz **kurz** lp: eterna 885 090
horn concerto damm

185/november 1974/lukaskirche/eterna sessions
meyer **müller-sybel** lp: eterna 885 028
des siegers dresden opera
gewissheit chorus
for tenor, schröter
chorus and
orchestra

peter schreier **rotzsch** lp: eterna 826 697
singt schreier
weihnachts-
lieder

186/22-24 february 1975/lukaskirche/eterna sessions
beethoven **blomstedt** lp: eterna 826 844
symphony cd: berlin classics BC 21982/BC 21942
no 7

187/17-18 march 1975/lukaskirche/eterna sessions
mozart **suitner** lp: eterna 826 852
symphony
no 40

mozart **suitner** lp: eterna 826 715
flute and walter cd: berlin classics BC 31652
harp concerto zoff

188/april 1975/lukaskirche/eterna sessions
kurz **kurz** lp: eterna 885 090
concerto for sandau cd: berlin classics BC 90692
trumpet and
strings

189/june 1975/lukaskirche/eterna-philips sessions
these sessions replaced a recording of verdi's un ballo in maschera, which was cancelled at short notice
verdi **varviso** lp: eterna 826 750
attila wixell lp: philips 6580 171
excerpt
(dagli immortali
vertici);
rigoletto excerpt
(cortigiani!);
la forza del
destino excerpt
(urna fatale);
un ballo in
maschera excerpt
(eri tu);
otello excerpt
(credo in un dio);
il trovatore
excerpt
(il balen);
don carlo
excerpt
(per me giunto);
falstaff excerpt
(e segno o realta)

wagner **varviso** lp: eterna 826 751
meistersinger; lp: philips 6570 030/6580 299
tannhäuser;
holländer
overtures;
lohengrin act 3
prelude;
tristan prelude

190/1-9 september 1975/lukaskirche/eterna-emi sessions

strauss violin concerto	**kempe** hoelscher	lp: eterna 826 553 lp: emi SLS 5067/1C191 02743-02746 lp: angel 32767 cd: emi CMS 764 3462/CZS 573 6142
strauss burleske for piano and orchestra	**kempe** frager	lp: eterna 826 553 lp: emi SLS 5067/1C191 02743-02746 lp: angel 32767 cd: emi CMS 764 3422/CZS 573 6142
parergon zur sinfonia domestica	**kempe** rösel	lp: eterna 826 856 lp: emi SLS 5067/1C191 02743-02746 cd: emi CMS 764 8422/CZS 573 6142
panathen- äenzug for piano and orchestra	**kempe** rösel	lp: eterna 826 856 lp: emi SLS 5067/1C191 02743-02746 cd: emi CMS 764 3422/CZS 573 6142

strauss
oboe concerto
	kempe
	clement
		lp: eterna 826 855
		lp: emi SLS 5067/1C191 02743-02746/
		    ESD 7026
		cd: emi CMS 764 3422/CDM 769 6612/
		    CZS 573 6142

strauss duett- concertino for clarinet and bassoon	**kempe** weise liebscher	lp: eterna 826 855 lp: emi SLS 5067/1C191 02743-02746 cd: emi CMS 764 3422/CDM 769 6612/ CZS 573 6142

strauss
horn concerti
nos 1
and 2
	kempe
	damm
		lp: eterna 826 854
		lp: emi SLS 5067/1C191 02743-02746/
		    1C063 02743
		lp: angel 37004
		cd: emi CMS 764 3422/CDM 769 6612/
		    CZS 573 6142

complete orchestral works of richard strauss under kempe also issued in usa by musical heritage society

191/september 1975/martin-luther-kirche/soundtrack recording for italian television (rai) film

rossini	**bertini**	lp: acanta JB 22308
l'italiana	dresden opera	cd: acanta 44.42308
in algeri	chorus	cd: austrophon 870 1622
	valentini-terrani	
	caputi	
	benelli	
	bruscantini	
	dara	
	mariotti	

192/october 1975/lukaskirche/eterna session

rosenfeld	**kurz**	lp: eterna 885 105
violin	schmahl	
concerto		
no 2		

193/1-7 december 1975/lukaskirche/eterna-emi sessions

bruckner	**jochum**	lp: eterna 827 533-827 534
symphony		lp: emi SLS 5252/1C127 54234-54244
no 4		cd: emi CZS 762 9352/CZS 573 9052/
"romantic"		CZS 574 8372

194/28-29 january 1976/lukaskirche/eterna sessions
kempe's final recordings with the orchestra

stravinsky	**kempe**	lp: eterna 827 012
l'oiseau de feu		cd: berlin classics BC 10972/BC 93942
suite (1919)		*also announced for publication by berlin classics in dvd audio format*

britten		lp: eterna 827 012
sinfonia		cd: berlin classics BC 10972
da requiem		*also announced for publication by berlin classics in dvd audio format*

195/17-21 march 1976/lukaskirche/eterna sessions

beethoven	lp: eterna
symphony	cd: berlin classics BC 21942/BC 21952
no 3	
"eroica"	

196/6-21 may 1976/lukaskirche/eterna-emi sessions

beethoven	**blomstedt**	lp: eterna 826 831-826 833
leonore	leipzig radio	lp: emi SLS 999/1C157 02853-02855
	chorus	cd: berlin classics BC 11402
	moser	*recording completed in june 1976*
	donath	
	cassilly	
	büchner	
	adam	
	ridderbusch	
	polster	

197/august 1976/lukaskirche/eterna sessions

köhler **kurz** lp: eterna 885 126
symphony
no 3

197a/15 august 1976/salzburg grosses festspielhaus/österreichischer rundfunk

beethoven **karajan** unpublished radio broadcast
piano concerto gilels
no 3;
shostakovich
symphony
no 10

198/24-29 august 1976/lukaskirche/eterna-emi sessions

strauss	**janowski**	lp: eterna 827 325-827 327
die schweigsame	dresden opera	lp: emi SLS 5160/1C165 03534-03536
frau	chorus	cd: emi CMS 566 0332
	scovotti	
	nossek	
	schmidt	
	burmeister	
	büchner	
	adam	
	schöne	

199/3-7 november 1976/lukaskirche/eterna-emi sessions

bruckner **jochum** lp: eterna 827 681-827 682
symphony lp: emi SLS 5147/SLS 5252/
no 8   1C157 03402-03403/1C127 54234-54244
      lp: angel 3893
      cd: emi CZS 762 9352/CZS 573 9052/
         CZS 573 8272

200/22-26 november 1976/lukaskirche/eterna sessions
mozart   **blomstedt**   lp: eterna 826 852
divertimenti   cd: ars vivendi 2100 215
k136, k137
and k138

201/11-14 december 1976/lukaskirche/eterna-emi sessions
bruckner   **jochum**   lp: eterna 827 537-827 538
symphony   lp: emi SLS 5194/SLS 5252/
no 7   1C157 03776-03777/1C127 54234-54244
                                lp: angel 3892
                                cd: emi CZS 762 9352/CZS 573 9052/
                                     CZS 568 6522

202/7 january 1977/kulturpalast/radio ddr
weiss   **kurz**   lp: eterna 885 209
concerto for   webersinke   cd: private issue HT 5306
organ, strings   *first performance of the work*
and percussion

203/january 1977/lukaskirche/eterna session
köhler   **kurz**   lp: eterns 885 126
piano   webersinke
concerto

204/23-27 january 1977/lukaskirche/eterna-emi sessions
bruckner   **jochum**   lp: eterna 827 138
symphony   lp: emi SLS 5252/ASD 4009/1C063 03598/
no 3   1C127 54234-54244
                                cd: emi CZS 762 9352/CZS 573 9052/
                                     CZS 568 6522

205/february 1977/lukaskirche/eterna sessions
schubert   **schreier**   lp: eterna 826 828
symphony   lp: eurodisc KK 25090
no 5   cd: berlin classics BC 30312
                                cd: corona classics CC 00992
                                also announced for publication by berlin
                                classics in dvd audio format

schubert   lp: eterna 826 828
symphony   lp: eurodisc KK 25090
no 8   cd: berlin classics BC 30312
"unfinished"   cd: corona classics CC 00662
                                also announced for publication by berlin
                                classics in dvd audio format

206/15 february 1977/lukaskirche/eterna session
mozart   **blomstedt**   lp: eterna 826 852
adagio and   cd: ars vivendi 2100 215
fugue
in c minor

207/1-5 march 1977/lukaskirche/eterna-emi sessions
schubert   **boskovsky**   lp: eterna 827 100
rosamunde   leipzig radio   lp: ASD 3498/1C063 02994/
incidental   chorus   2C069 02994
music   cotrubas   cd: berlin classics BC 90042
                                              overture
                                              cd: berlin classics BC 93942

208/14-18 march 1977/lukaskirche/eterna sessions
beethoven   **blomstedt**   lp: eterna 827 148
symphony   cd: berlin classics BC 21972/BC 21942
no 5

208a/24 march 1977/kulturpalast/radio ddr
beethoven   **blomstedt**   cd: private issue vienna
piano concerti   gilels
nos 4 and 5
"emperor"

209/6-9 may 1977/lukaskirche/eterna sessions
beethoven   **blomstedt**   lp: eterna 827 179
symphony   cd: berlin classics BC 21972/BC 21942
no 6
"pastoral"

210/9-10 and 23-24 june 1977/lukaskirche/eterna-emi sessions
grieg   **blomstedt**   lp: eterna 827 180
peer gynt   leipzig radio   lp: emi 1C063 03398
incidental   chorus   cd: emi CDZ 252 1192
music   valjakka   *recording completed in october 1977*
                      thallaug
joachim ulbricht, viola soloist

211/9-15 september 1977/lukaskirche/eterna-dg sessions

mozart	**böhm**	lp: eterna 827 277-827 280
idomeneo	leipzig radio chorus	lp: dg 2711 023/2740 195/ 2740 202/2740 222
	mathis	cd: dg 429 8642/435 3962
	varady	*excerpts*
	ochman	lp: eterna 827 160
	schreier	lp: dg 2537 051
	winkler	

212/september 1977/lukaskirche/eterna-dg sessions

mozart **klee** lp: eterna 827 174
exsultate mathis lp: dg 2530 978
jubilate; cd: berlin classics BC 91752
betracht dies herz; *recording completed in june 1978*
ein ergrimmter
löwe brüllt;
laudate dominum k321;
hat der schöpfer
dieses lebens;
quel nocchier
che in gran procella
hans otto, organ and harpsichord soloist

mozart **klee** lp: eterna 827 174
vesperae dresdner lp: dg 2530 978
solennes kapellknaben cd: berlin classics BC 91752
excerpt mathis
(laudate
dominum)

213/december 1977-january 1978/lukaskirche/eterna sessions

vivaldi concerto in f for 2 horns and orchestra; reicha concerto for 2 horns and orchestra	**kurz** damm vincze	lp: eterna 827 873
fick horn concerto in e flat; sperger horn concerto in e flat	**kurz** damm	lp: eterna 827 873
tchaikovsky symphony no 5	**kurz**	lp: eterna 827 376 cd: ars vivendi 2253 104

214/11-13 january 1978/lukaskirche/eterna-emi sessions

bruckner **jochum** lp: eterna 827 197
symphony lp: emi SLS 5252/ASD 4218/
no 9 EG 29 04921/1C063 43197/
 1C127 54234-54244
 lp: angel 34736/37700
 cd: emi CZS 762 9352/CZS 573 9052/
 CZS 573 8272

215/14-16 february 1978/lukaskirche/eterna sessions

beethoven **blomstedt** lp: eterna 827 422
symphony cd: berlin classics BC 21982/BC 21942
no 8

216/6-13 march 1978/lukaskirche/eterna-emi sessions
smetana   **berglund**   lp: eterna 827 199-827 200
ma vlast   lp: emi SLS 5151/1C161 03470-03471
                                       cd: emi CDR 573 5212/CZS 568 6492

dvorak   lp: eterna 827 199-827 200
slavonic   lp: emi SLS 5151/1C161 03470-03471
rhapsody no 3;   cd: emi CZS 568 6492
scherzo
capriccioso

217/20-24 march 1978/lukaskirche/eterna sessions
schubert   **blomstedt**   lp: eterna 827 551
symphony   cd: berlin classics BC 92662
no 3

schubert   lp: eterna 827 679
symphony   cd: ars vivendi 2100 109
no 8
"unfinished"

218/9-13 june 1978/lukaskirche/eterna-emi sessions
bruckner   **jochum**   lp: eterna 827 535
symphony   lp: emi SLS 5252/ASD 4080/
no 6   1C127 54234-54244
                                   lp: angel 37695
                                   cd: emi CZS252 9352/CZS 573 9052/
                                          CZS 572 6612

219/2-6 july 1978/lukaskirche/eterna-emi sessions

mendelssohn	**janowski**	lp: eterna 827 159
violin	hoelscher	lp: emi 1C063 03647
concerto		cd: berlin classics BC 93942

schumann		lp: eterna 827 159
violin		lp: emi 1C063 03647
concerto		

220/21-24 august 1978/lukaskirche/eterna sessions

beethoven	**blomstedt**	lp: eterna 827 158
symphony		cd: berlin classics BC 21962/BC 21942
no 4		

221/25 august 1978/lukaskirche/eterna session
recordings in this session were completed in october and november 1978

wagner	**janowski**	lp: eterna 827 045
das rheingold	adam	lp: eurodisc 300 319.420
excerpt		
(abendlich		
strahlt der		
sonne auge)		

wagner	**janowski**	lp: eterna 827 045
die walküre	schröter	lp: eurodisc 300 319.420
excerpt	adam	
(lass ich's		
verlauten)		

wagner	**janowski**	lp: eterna 827 045
siegfried	lahusen-oertel	lp: eurodisc 300 319.420
excerpt	adam	
(wala erwache!)		

wagner	**janowski**	lp: eterna 827 045
parsifal	schreier	lp: eurodisc 300 319.420
excerpt	adam	
(du wuschest		
mir die füsse)		

222/8-12 november 1978/lukaskirche/eterna-emi sessions

mozart	**blomstedt**	lp: eterna 827 382
concert arias:	moser	lp: emi 1C063 29082
ah lo previdi;		*lp also included mozart operatic arias*
popoli di		*accompanied by other orchestras and conductors*
tessaglia!;		
mia speranza		
adorata; schon		
lacht der holde		
frühling		

223/11-15 december 1978/lukaskirche/eterna-emi sessions

bruckner	**jochum**	lp: eterna 827 426
symphony		lp: emi SLS 5252/ASD 3825/1C063 03716/
no 1		2C127 54234-54244
		cd: emi CZS 762 9352/CZS 573 9052

224/12 january 1979/kulturpalast/radio ddr

schubert	**böhm**	lp: eterna 827 157
symphony		lp: dg 2531 352/419 4841
no 9		cd: dg 419 4842
"great"		*recorded at böhm's final public appearance with the orchestra in dresden; also unpublished video recording of rehearsal fragment*

225/16-24 january 1979/lukaskirche/eterna-dg sessions

mozart	**böhm**	lp: eterna 827 379-827 381
la clemenza	leipzig radio	lp: dg 2709 092/2740 208/2740 222
di tito	chorus	cd: dg 429 8782/435 3962
	mathis	*excerpts*
	varady	lp: dg 2537 054
	berganza	cd: dg 459 3902
	schiml	*recording completed in march 1979*
	schreier	
	adam	

orchestral soloists: joachim mäder, clarinet; rolf schindler, basset horn

Staatskapelle Dresden
Chefdirigent Herbert Blomstedt

Freitag, 12. Januar 1979, 20 Uhr
Sonnabend, 13. Januar 1979, 17 Uhr
Kulturpalast

Dirigent
Karl Böhm

1. Sonderkonzert

Franz Schubert (1797–1828)
Sinfonie Nr. 8, h-Moll („Unvollendete")
Allegro moderato
Andante con moto

Pause

Sinfonie Nr. 7, C-Dur
Andante – Allegro ma non troppo
Andante con moto
Scherzo. Allegro vivace
Finale. Allegro vivace

226/february 1979/katholische hofkirche

hasse	**wagner**	cd: christophorus CHR 74531
regina coeli;	dresdner	
gloria from	kapellknaben	
mass in	ihle	
d minor	pfretzschner	
	ude	

227/march 1979/lukaskirche/eterna sessions

schubert	**gülke**	lp: eterna 827 934
three		cd: ars vivendi 2100 216
symphonic		
fragments		
arranged		
by gülke		

mozart	**blomstedt**	lp: eterna 827 932
concert arias:	scovotti	
misero pargoletto!;		
voi avete un cor fedele;		
ma che vi fece o stelle!;		
a questo seno deh vieni;		
no che non sei capace;		
ah se in ciel benigne stelle!;		
chi sa chi sa qual sia!		

228/9-11 april 1979/lukaskirche/eterna sessions

beethoven	**blomstedt**	lp: eterna 827 524-827 525
symphony	dresden opera	lp: victor RL 30440
no 9	chorus	cd: berlin classics BC 21992/BC 21942
"choral"	doese	*recording completed in march 1980; also*
	schiml	*announced for publication by berlin classics*
	schreier	*in dvd audio format*
	adam	

229/april 1979/lukaskirche/eterna sessions
j.strauss **wallberg** lp: eterna 845 163
eine nacht in   lp: eurodisc 200 545.366
venedig overture;
wo die zitronen
blüh'n waltz;
czardas from
ritter pasman;
neue pizzicato polka;
komzak
bad'ner madln;
ziehrer
hereinspaziert;
ochs variations on
's kommt ein
vogel geflogen

229a/24-25 may 1979/schauspielhaus/ddr television
jochum's final public concert with the orchestra
brahms   **jochum**   unpublished video recording
piano concerto   béroff
no 2

brahms   **jochum**   cd: meteor (japan) MCD 046
symphony   *also unpublished video recording*
no 4

230/17-19 september 1979/lukaskirche/eterna sessions
schubert   **blomstedt**   lp: eterna 827 552
symphony   cd: berlin classics BC 90242
no 6

231/24 october 1979/new york united nations building/tv transmission
beethoven   **blomstedt**   unpublished video recording
symphony   l.price
no 8;
matthus responso;
wagner
meistersinger
von nürnberg
overture;
strauss 4 letzte lieder

232/3-7 december 1979/lukaskirche/eterna sessions
j.strauss   **suitner**   lp: eterna
an der schönen   cd: ars vivendi 2153 121
blauen donau
annen polka;
vergnügungszug;
eljen a magyar;
unter donner
und blitz;
künstlerleben;
freikugeln;
j.strauss father
radetzky march;
josef strauss
dorfschwalben
aus österreich;
mein lebenslauf
ist lieb' und lust

233/19-21 december 1979/lukaskirche/eterna sessions
beethoven   **blomstedt**   lp: eterna 827 422
symphony   cd: berlin classics BC 21952/BC 21492
no 1

beethoven   lp: eterna 827 525
symphony   cd: berlin classics BC 21962/BC 21492
no 2

234/22-27 january 1980/lukaskirche/eterna-emi sessions
bruckner   **jochum**   lp: eterna 827 531
symphony   lp: emi SLS 5252/ASD 4081/1C063 43097/
no 2   1C127 54234-54244
                                cd: emi CZS 762 9352/CZS 573 9052/
                                   CZS 574 8372

235/25 february-3 march 1980/lukaskirche/eterna-emi sessions
bruckner   **jochum**   lp: eterna 827 737-827 738
symphony   lp: emi SLS 5252/1C127 54234-54244
no 5   cd: emi CZS 762 9352/CZS 573 9052/
                                   CZS 572 6612

complete bruckner symphonies under jochum also issued in usa by musical heritage society

236/19-21 march 1980/lukaskirche/eterna sessions
schubert   **blomstedt**   lp: eterna 827 552
symphony   cd: ars vivendi 2100 109
no 5   *recording completed in april and october 1980*

237/8-10 april 1980/lukaskirche/eterna session
rimsky-korsakov **janowski**   lp: eterna
mozart and   leipzig radio   cd: berlin classics BC 20892
salieri   chorus
                          schreier
                          adam
                          sung in german

238/17-19 may 1980/lukaskirche/eterna sessions
schubert   **blomstedt**   lp: eterna 827 551
symphony   cd: berlin classics BC 92662
no 4
"tragic"

239/30 june-7 july 1980/lukaskirche/eterna sessions
bruckner   **blomstedt**   lp: eterna 729 268
symphony   cd: denon 38C37-7286
no 7

240/july 1980/katholische hofkirche/radio ddr
hasse   **wagner**   cd: christophorus CHR 74531
te deum   dresdner
                        kapellknaben
                        ihle
                        pfretzschner
                        ude

241/august 1980/lukaskirche/eterna-dg sessions

wagner	**kleiber**	lp: eterna 827 577-827 581
tristan und	leipzig radio	lp: dg 2741 006
isolde	chorus	cd: dg 413 3152
	m.price	*excerpts*
	fassbänder	lp: dg 410 5341
	kollo	cd: dg 459 3902
	dermota	*recording completed in october 1980 and*
	fischer-dieskau	*february and april 1981*
	moll	

manfred krause, cor anglais soloist

242/8-12 september 1980/lukaskirche/eterna sessions

mozart	**blomstedt**	lp: eterna 827 646
concert arias:	schreier	
va dal furor;		
tali e cotanti;		
simostro la sorte;		
con ossequio;		
clarice cara		
mia sposa;		
se al labbro;		
per pieta non		
ricercate;		
misero s sogno!		

243/6-10 october 1980/lukaskirche/eterna sessions

schubert	**blomstedt**	lp: eterna 827 649
symphony		cd: berlin classics BC 92632
no 2		

244/8-11 december 1980/lukaskirche/eterna-eurodisc sessions

wagner	**janowski**	lp: eterna 827 582-827 584
das rheingold	napier	lp: eurodisc 301 137
	minton	cd: eurodisc 610 058
	wenkel	cd: rca/bmg GD 69004/GD 69003/
	schreier	74321 454 182/74321 454 172
	büchner	*excerpts*
	c.vogel	lp: eterna 827 045/729 270
	adam	*also unpublished radio broadcast of the concert*
	nimsgern	*performance which took place in dresden at the*
	stryczek	*time of these sessions*
	bracht	
	salminen	

245/23-27 march 1981/lukaskirche/eterna sessions

schubert	**blomstedt**	lp: eterna 827 679-827 680
symphony		cd: ars vivendi 2100 113
no 9		cd: berlin classics BC 93142
"great"		*also issued in japan by deutsche schallplatten and on a pickwick label entitled orchid, where it is incorrectly described as a performance conducted by eugen jochum with the berlin radio orchestra*

246/april-may 1981/lukaskirche/eterna sessions

boieldieu	**kurz**	lp: eterna 827 684
harp concerto	zoff	cd: ars vivendi 2100 167
in c;		
ginastera		
harp concerto		

247/14-15 may 1981/lukaskirche/eterna sessions

reger	**blomstedt**	lp: eterna 827 686
violin	scherzer	cd: berlin classics BC 91242
concerto		

schubert	**blomstedt**	lp: eterna 827 649
symphony		cd: berlin classics BC 92632
no 1		

248/4 june 1981/lukaskirche/eterna session

tchaikovsky	**vonk**	lp: eterna 827 655
violin	funke	cd: ars vivendi 2253 104
concerto		cd: berlin classics BC 93842
		recording completed in july 1981

249/14-18 august 1981/lukaskirche/eterna-denon sessions
mozart   **blomstedt**   lp: eterna 827 667
symphony   cd: denon DC 8082/38C37-7022
no 40;
symphony
no 41
"jupiter"

250/22-29 august 1981/lukaskirche/eterna-eurodisc sessions
wagner   **janowski**   lp: eterna 827 585-827 589
die walküre   altmeyer   lp: eurodisc 301 143
                 norman   cd: eurodisc 610 064
                 minton   cd: rca/bmg GD 69005/GD 69003/
                 jerusalem   74321 454192/74321 454172
                 adam   *excerpts*
                 moll   lp: eterna 827 045/729 271
                                   also unpublished radio broadcast of the concert performance which took place in dresden at the time of these sessions

251/7-11 september 1981/lukaskirche/eterna-denon sessions
bruckner   **blomstedt**   lp: eterna 725 007
symphony   cd: denon 38C37-7126
no 4
"romantic"

252/31 october-3 november 1981/lukaskirche/eterna-philips sessions

mozart	**davis**	lp: eterna 827 668/729 260
symphony		lp: philips 6514 206
no 28		cd: deutsche schallplatten 329 260
		cd: philips 426 2362

mozart	lp: eterna 827 792/729 248
symphony	lp: philips 6514 205
no 29	cd: deutsche schallplatten 329 248
	cd: philips 426 2362

mozart	lp: eterna 827 792/729 248
symphony	lp: philips 6514 205
no 39	cd: deutsche schallplatten 329 248
	cd: philips 410 0462

mozart	lp: eterna 827 668/729 260
symphony	lp: philips 6514 206
no 41	cd: deutsche schallplatten 329 260
"jupiter"	cd: philips 410 0462

253/december 1981/lukaskirche/eterna sessions

mozart **blomstedt** lp: eterna 827 755
concert arias: scovotti
a berenice;
non curo l'affetto;
fra cento affanni;
alcandro lo
confesso;
non so d'onde
viene;
vorrei spiegarvi

wolfgang holzhäuser, oboe soloist in vorrei spiegarvi

Staatskapelle Dresden

Chefdirigent Herbert Blomstedt
Dienstag, 30. März 1982
18 Uhr, Kulturpalast

Opernkonzert

*In Zusammenarbeit
mit dem VEB Deutsche
Schallplatten Berlin*

Richard Wagner
Siegfried

Siegfried	René Kollo
Mime	Heinz Zednik
Der Wanderer	Theo Adam
Alberich	Siegmund Nimsgern
Fafner	Matti Salminen
Erda	Ortrun Wenkel
Brünnhilde	Jeannine Altmeyer
Stimme eines Waldvogels	Norma Sharp
Hornsolo	Peter Damm
Musikalische Assistenz	Gottfried Hämpel

DIRIGENT
MAREK JANOWSKI

Pausen nach dem 1. und 2. Aufzug

254/february-march 1982/lukaskirche/eterna-eurodisc sessions

wagner	**janowski**	lp: eterna 827 590-827 594
siegfried	altmeyer	lp: eurodisc 301 810
	sharp	cd: eurodisc 610 070
	wenkel	cd: rca/bmg GD 69006/GD 69003/
	kollo	74321 454202/74321 454 172
	schreier	*excerpts*
	adam	lp: eterna 827 045/827 888
	nimsgern	*also unpublished radio broadcast of the concert*
	salminen	*performance which took place in dresden at the time of these sessions*

255/12-16 april 1982/lukaskirche/eterna-philips sessions

mozart	**schreier**	lp: eterna 729 249
requiem	leipzig radio	lp: philips 6514 320
	chorus	cd: philips 411 4202/464 7202
	m.price	
	schmidt	
	araiza	
	adam	

256/may 1982/lukaskirche/eterna session

mozart	**blomstedt**	lp: eterna 827 755
concert arias:	moser	
misera dove son?;		
bella mia fiamma		

257/15 june 1982/venice teatro la fenice

strauss	**kurz**	cd: mondo musica MFOH 10707
rosenkavalier	dresden opera	*guest performance given by staatsoper dresden;*
	chorus	*mondo musica incorrectly name singer of the*
	zobel	*role of ochs as theo adam*
	höhne	
	trekel-burkhardt	
	könig	
	haseleu	
	haunstein	

RICHARD STRAUSS
Il Cavaliere della Rosa
Staatskapelle Dresden - Coro Staatsoper Dresden
Direttore Siegfried Kurz

Ingeborg Zobel
Theo Adam
Ute Trekel-Burckhardt

Rolf Haunstein
Barbara Hoene

258/25 june-1 july 1982/lukaskirche/eterna-philips sessions

elgar	**marriner**	lp: eterna 827 759
cello concerto	schiff	lp: philips 6514 316
		cd: philips 412 8802

elgar	**marriner**	lp: eterna 827 759
introduction		lp: philips 6514 316
and allegro		
for strings		

orchestral soloists: peter mirring and wolfram just, violins; peter schikora, viola; gerhard pluswik, cello

elgar	lp: eterna 827 759
cockaigne	lp: philips 6514 316
overture	

tchaikovsky	lp: eterna 729 264
capriccio	lp: philips 410 0471
italien;	cd: philips 410 0472
glinka	
caprice	
brillant;	
chabrier	
espana;	
ravel	
boléro	

259/1-3 september 1982/lukaskirche/eterna-denon sessions

mozart	**blomstedt**	lp: eterna 827 941
symphony		cd: denon 38C37-7146/DC 8081
no 38		
"prague";		
symphony		
no 39		

260/november 1982/lukaskirche/eterna sessions
mozart	**kurz**	lp: eterna
clarinet	michallik	cd: berlin classics BC 31072
concerto		

mozart	**kurz**	lp: eterna
bassoon	klier	cd: berlin classics BC 31652
concerto		

261/5 march 1983/katholische hofkirche
zelenka	**wagner**	cd: christophorus CHR 74550
missa	dresdner	
circumcisionis	kapellknaben	
	ihle	
	pfretzschner	
	wagner	
	henneberg	

262/april 1983/lukaskirche/eterna-eurodisc sessions
wagner	**janowski**	lp: eterna 827 595-827 599
götter-	dresden opera	lp: eurodisc 301 817
dämmerung	chorus	cd: eurodisc 610 081
	altmeyer	cd: rca/bmg GD 69007/GD 69003/
	sharp	74321 454212/74321 454172
	wenkel	*excerpts*
	kollo	lp: eterna 827 889
	nöcker	*also unpublished radio broadcast of the concert*
	nimsgern	*performance which took place in dresden at the*
	salminen	*time of these sessions*

263/june 1983/lukaskirche/eterna session
martin	**kurz**	lp: eterna
ballade	walter	cd: berlin classics BC 91612
for flute		
and strings		

264/june-july 1983/lukaskirche/eterna sessions

weber concertino for horn and orchestra	**kurz** damm	lp: eterna 827 873 cd: berlin classics BC 93242
lortzing konzertstück for horn and orchestra		lp: eterna 827 873 cd: berlin classics BC 93242
saint-saens morceau de concert for horn and orchestra		lp: eterna 827 873 cd: berlin classics BC 93242
schumann konzertstück for 4 horns	**kurz** damm pietzonka pansa friemel	lp: eterna 827 873 cd: berlin classics BC 93242

265/november-december 1983/lukaskirche/eterna-philips sessions

verdi	**varviso**	lp: eterna 827 874
nabucco	dresden opera	lp: philips 412 2351
excerpts	chorus	cd: philips 412 2352
(va pensiero!;		
gli arredi festivi);		
il trovatore		
excerpts		
(vedi le fosche;		
or co' dadi);		
aida excerpt		
(gloria all'egitto!);		
i lombardi excerpta		
(gerusalem!;		
o signore!);		
macbeth excerpt		
(patria oppressa);		
otello excerpt		
(fuoco di gioia!);		
don carlo excerpt		
(spuntato ecco il di		
d'esultanza)		

265/concluded
bizet carmen prelude;	**varviso**	lp: eterna 725 009
mascagni cavalleria rusticana intermezzo;		lp: philips 412 2361
		cd: deutsche schallplatten 329 009
		cd: philips 412 2362/454 4862

ponchielli
la gioconda
dance of the hours;
puccini
manon lescaut
intermezzo;
rossini
la gazza ladra
intermezzo;
schmidt
notre dame
intermezzo;
massenet thais
méditation;
offenbach
les contes d'hoffmann
barcarolle;
saint-saens
samson et dalila
bacchanale

266/2-11 january 1984/lukaskirche/eterna-philips sessions
mozart zauberflöte	**davis** leipzig radio chorus m.price serra venuti schreier melbye moll	lp: eterna 725 027-725 029
		lp: philips 411 4591
		cd: philips 411 4592/422 5432/442 5682/ 464 6602/464 9302
		excerpts
		cd: philips 432 6182/446 2472/464 6482
		442 5682 omits spoken dialogue

267/25 february-1 march 1984/lukaskirche/eterna-teldec sessions

mozart	**harnoncourt**	lp: eterna 725 003
serenade no 7	zehetmair	lp: teldec AZ 643.062
"haffner";		cd: deutsche schallplatten 329 003
march		cd: teldec 4509 959862/2292 430402/
in d k249		9031 724812/4509 986922

mozart	**harnoncourt**	lp: eterna 725 011
serenade no 9	damm	lp: teldec AZ 643.063
"posthorn";		cd: deutsche schallplatten 329 011
marches in d		cd: teldec 4509 921492/4509 959862/
k335 nos		2292 430402/9031 724812
1 and 2		

268/25 april 1984/kulturpalast/radio ddr

weiss	**blomstedt**	lp: eterna 885 290
symphony		
no 3		

269/august-september 1984/lukaskirche/eterna-philips sessions

bach	**schreier**	lp: eterna 725 113-725 115
matthäus-	dresdner	lp: philips 412 5271
passion	kapellknaben	cd: philips 412 5272/454 1082
	leipzig radio	*excerpts*
	chorus	lp: eterna 729 267
	popp	lp: philips 420 8481
	lipovsek	cd: philips 420 8482
	schreier	
	büchner	
	holl	
	adam	
	scheibner	
	wlaschiha	
	polster	
	bär	

orchestral soloists: johannes walter, wilfried gärtner, eckhart haupt, gudrun jahn, arndt schöne and ulrich philipp, flutes; kurt mahn, manfred krause, peter thieme, andreas lorenz and wolfgang klier, oboes; peter mirring and roland straumer, violins; siegfried pank, viola da gamba; ernst-ludwig hammer and günter müller, cellos; gerhard neumerkel and werner zeibig, double basses; wolfgang liebscher and günter klier, bassoons; walter-heinz bernstein and christine schornsheim, organs

270/september 1984/lukaskirche/eterna-emi sessions

weber	**blomstedt**	lp: eterna 827 957
piano concerti	rösel	lp: emi EL 27 03581
nos 1 and 2;		cd: berlin classics BC 10582
konzertstück		
for piano and		
orchestra		

271/10-14 october 1984/lukaskirche/eterna-denon sessions

strauss	**blomstedt**	lp: eterna 725 066
ein heldenleben		cd: denon 38C37-7561
peter mirring, violin soloist		cd: laserlight COCO 75005

272/15-23 november 1984/lukaskirche/eterna-philips sessions

fauré	**davis**	lp: eterna 725 079
requiem	leipzig radio	lp: philips 412 7431
	chorus	cd: deutsche schallplatten 329 079
	popp	cd: philips 412 7432
	estes	

beethoven	**davis**	lp: eterna 729 214
piano concerto	arrau	lp: philips 416 1441
no 4		cd: deutsche schallplatten 329 214
		cd: philips 416 1442/422 1492/464 6812

beethoven		lp: eterna 729 083
piano concerto		lp: philips 416 2151
no 5		cd: deutsche schallplatten 329 083
"emperor"		cd: philips 416 2152/422 1492/464 6812
		cd: dg 459 3902

273/3-5 december 1984/lukaskirche/eterna-emi sessions
beethoven	**vonk**	lp: eterna 827 958
violin	hoelscher	lp: emi EL 27 02781
concerto		cd: emi CDM 769 0982/CMS 763 9372

274/17-21 december 1984/lukaskirche/eterna sessions
wagner	**wakasugi**	lp: eterna 725 037
der fliegende		cd: deutsche schallplatten 329 037
holländer		cd: berlin classics BC 11522
overture		cd: corona classics CC 00112

wagner		lp: eterna 725 037
tannhäuser;		cd: deutsche schallplatten 329 037
rienzi overtures;		cd: berlin classics BC 11522
lohengrin		
preludes		
acts 1 and 3		

275/13 february 1985/semperoper/eterna-denon live recording
weber	**hauschild**	lp: eterna 827 913-827 915
der freischütz	dresden opera	cd: denon 38C37 7433-7435
	chorus	*opening performance in the re-built semperoper*
	smitkova	
	ihle	
	goldberg	
	ketelsen	
	emmerlich	
	adam	

orchestral soloists: joachim zindler, viola; clemens dillner, cello

276/14 february 1985/semperoper/eterna-denon live recording
strauss	**vonk**	lp: eterna 827 916-827 919
rosenkavalier	dresden opera	cd: denon 38C37 7482-7484
	chorus	*second performance in the re-built semperoper;*
	pusar	*also unpublished video recording*
	stejskal	
	walther	
	könig	
	adam	
	haunstein	

277/march 1985/lukaskirche/eterna-capriccio sessions
weber   **kuhn**   lp: eterna 827 955
abu hassan;   lp: capriccio C 27076
beherrscher   cd: capriccio 10052
der geister;
euryanthe;
der freischütz;
jubel; oberon;
preciosa;
turandot
overtures

tchaikovsky   **vonk**   lp: eterna 725 076-725 077
casse noisette   cd: capriccio 10071-10072/51009
ballet;
evgeny onegin
waltz, polonaise
and mazurka

278/30-31 march 1985/semperoper/eterna-capriccio live recording
beethoven   **blomstedt**   lp: eterna 827 920-827 921
symphony   dresden opera   cd: capriccio 10060
no 9   chorus   cd: laserlight COCO 78030
"choral"   wiens   *performed as part of the celebrations marking*
                      walther   *opening of re-built semperoper*
                      goldberg
                      stryczek

279/20-24 april 1985/lukaskirche/eterna-emi sessions

haydn	**marriner**	lp: eterna 725 039/729 039
mass no 10	leipzig radio	lp: emi EL 27 04131
"missa in	chorus	cd: deutsche schallplatten 329 039
tempore	marshall	cd: emi CDC 747 4252
belli"	watkinson	
	lewis	
	holl	

clemens dillner, cello soloist

haydn	lp: eterna 725 040/729 040
mass no 11	lp: emi EL 27 04121
"nelson	cd: deutsche schallplatten 329 040
mass"	cd: emi CDC 747 4242/CZS 568 5922/
	CMS 566 3322

280/20-24 june 1985/lukaskirche/eterna sessions

beethoven	**wakasugi**	lp: eterna 729 168
symphony		cd: deutsche schallplatten 329 168
no 3		
"eroica"		

281/25-28 june 1985/lukaskirche/eterna-emi sessions

mozart	**zinman**	lp: eterna 729 047
piano concerto	zacharias	lp: emi EL 27 03671
no 22		cd: deutsche schallplatten 329 047
		cd: emi CDC 747 4282

mozart	lp: eterna 729 047
piano concerto	lp: emi EL 27 03671
no 23	cd: deutsche schallplatten 329 047
	cd: emi CDC 747 4282/CZS 767 5612/
	CDM 763 9012

282/july 1985/lukaskirche/eterna-capriccio sessions

mozart	**vonk**	lp: eterna 725 057/729 057
overtures:		lp: capriccio C 27086
ascanio in alba;		cd: deutsche schallplatten 329 057
lucio silla;		cd: capriccio 10070
idomeneo; finta		
giardiniera;		
clemenza di tito;		
entführung		
aus dem serail;		
cosi fan tutte;		
schauspieldirektor;		
don giovanni;		
le nozze di figaro;		
die zauberflöte		

283/september 1985/lukaskirche/eterna-emi sessions

weber	**blomstedt**	lp: eterna 725 067/729 067
clarinet	meyer	lp: emi EL 27 03591
concerti		cd: deutsche schallplatten 329 067
nos 1 and 2;		cd: emi CDC 747 3512
concertino		
for clarinet		
and orchestra		

284/23 february-3 march 1986/lukaskirche/eterna-emi sessions

beethoven	**tate**	lp: eterna 725 140/729 140
symphony		lp: emi EL 27 05441
no 7;		cd: deutsche schallplatten 329 140
die weihe		cd: emi CDC 747 8152
des hauses		
overture		
schubert		lp: eterna 725 177/729 177
symphony		lp: emi EL 27 05001
no 9		lp: angel 38336
"great"		cd: deutsche schallplatten 329 177
		cd: emi CDC 747 4782
		cd: berlin classics BC 10832

285/june 1986/lukaskirche/eterna sessions
auber	**vonk**	lp: eterna
fra diavolo;		cd: ars vivendi 2100 136/MRC 036
flotow martha;		
alessandro stradella;		
lortzing zar und zimmermann;		
nicolai lustige weiber von windsor;		
adam si j'étais roi;		
cornelius barbier von bagdad;		
reznicek donna diana		
overtures		

286/23-29 august 1986/lukaskirche/eterna sessions
mahler	**wakasugi**	lp: eterna 725 119/729 119
symphony no 1		cd: deutsche schallplatten 329 119

287/14-19 september 1986/lukaskirche/eterna-emi sessions
haydn	**marriner**	lp: eterna 725 109/729 109
mass no 12	leipzig radio	cd: deutsche schallplatten 329 109
"theresien-	chorus	cd: emi CDC 749 0722/CZS 568 5922/
messe"	vaness	CMS 566 3322
	soffel	
	lewis	
	salomaa	
haydn	**marriner**	cd: emi CDC 749 0722/CZS 568 5922/
mass no 9	leipzig radio	CMS 566 3322
"heiligmesse"	chorus	
	vaness	
	schellenberger	
	lewis	
	salomaa	
	polster	

288/30 september-3 october 1986/lukaskirche/eterna-emi sessions

beethoven	**vonk**	cd: emi CDC 749 2302/CMS 763 9372
piano concerto	zacharias	
no 2		

beethoven		cd: emi CDC 749 2302/CMS 763 9372/
piano concerto		CDE 574 5562
no 4		

289/21 november-5 december 1986/lukaskirche/eterna-philips sessions

bach	**schreier**	lp: eterna 725 159-725 161
weihnachts-	leipzig radio	lp: philips 420 2041
oratorium	chorus	cd: philips 420 2042/454 1082
	donath	*excerpts*
	ihle	lp: eterna 725 162/729 162
	schreier	*recording completed in january 1987*
	büchner	
	holl	

orchestral soloists: peter mirring and reinhard ulbricht, violins; joachim bischof, cello; werner zeibig, double bass; eckart haupt and ulrich philipp, flutes; wolfgang holzhäuser, bernhard mühlbach, andreas lorenz, wolfgang klier, manfred krause and peter thieme, oboes; günter klier, bassoon; peter damm and dieter pansa, horns; ludwig güttler, mathias schmutzler and roland rudolph, trumpets; christine schornsheim, organ; raphael alpermann, harpsichord

290/6-11 february 1987/lukaskirche/eterna-philips sessions

beethoven	**davis**	lp: eterna 725 212/729 212
piano concerto	arrau	lp: philips 422 0661
no 1		cd: deutsche schallplatten 329 212
		cd: philips 422 0662/422 1492

beethoven		lp: eterna 725 213/729 213
piano concerto		lp: philips 422 1481
no 3		cd: deutsche schallplatten 329 213
		cd: philips 422 1482/422 1492

291/june 1987/lukaskirche/eterna-dg sessions

tchaikovsky	**levine**	lp: dg 423 9591
evgeny	leipzig radio	cd: dg 423 9592
onegin	chorus	*excerpts*
	freni	cd: dg 427 6812/445 4672/459 3902/
	otter	469 5882
	schicoff	
	allen	
	burchuladze	

292/22-26 june 1987/lukaskirche/eterna-denon sessions

strauss	**blomstedt**	lp: eterna 725 226/729 226
also sprach		cd: deutsche schallplatten 329 226
zarathustra		cd: denon CO 2259

torsten janicke, violin soloist

293/26 june-7 july 1987/lukaskirche/eterna-philips sessions

offenbach	**tate**	lp: philips 422 3741
les contes	leipzig radio	cd: philips 422 3742
d'hoffmann	chorus	*excerpts*
	norman	cd: philips 438 5022
	studer	*recording completed in july 1988 and june 1989*
	lind	
	otter	
	araiza	
	ramey	

294/16 august 1987/lukaskirche/eterna-denon session

strauss	**blomstedt**	lp: eterna 725 226/729 226
don juan		cd: deutsche schallplatten 329 226
		cd: denon CO 2259

295/september 1987/lukaskirche/eterna-dg sessions

bruckner	**sinopoli**	lp: eterna 725 216/729 216
symphony		lp: dg 423 6771
no 4		cd: deutsche schallplatten 329 216
"romantic"		cd: dg 423 6772
		sinopoli's first recording with the orchestra

296/7 october 1987/berlin schauspielhaus/radio ddr
krätzschmar   **vonk**   cd: wergo LC 0846
cataracta per
orchestra

297/13-14 october 1987/lukaskirche/eterna-philips sessions
beethoven   **davis**   lp: eterna 725 214/729 214
piano concerto   arrau   lp: philips 422 0661
no 2   cd: deutsche schallplatten 329 214
                                       cd: philips 422 0662/422 1492

298/10-12 january 1988/lukaskirche/eterns-emi sessions
beethoven   **vonk**   cd: emi CDC 749 3722/CMS 763 9372/
piano concerto   zacharias   CDE 574 5562
no 5
"emperor"

299/15-17 january 1988/lukaskirche/eterna-philips sessions
recordings in these sessions were completed in january 1989
mozart   **schreier**   cd: philips 426 2732
mass in   leipzig radio
c minor   chorus
"great"   hendricks
                    coburn
                    blochwitz
                    schmidt

299/concluded

mozart coronation mass	**schreier** leipzig radio chorus mathis rappé blochwitz quasthoff	cd: philips 426 2752/464 7202
mozart vesperae solennes de conhessore		cd: philips 426 2752
mozart ave verum corpis	**schreier** leipzig radio chorus	cd: philips 426 2752/464 7202 *464 7202 dates this recording as june 1992*
mozart laut verkünde uns're freude cantata		cd: philips 426 8962/464 6602/464 8702
mozart die maurerfreude cantata		cd: philips 422 5222/464 6602/464 8702
mozart dir seele des weltalls cantata	**schreier** leipzig radio chorus blochwitz	cd: philips 422 5222/464 6602/464 8702
mozart maurerische trauermusik	**schreier**	cd: philips 422 5222/446 2402/ 464 6602/464 8702

300/february 1988/lukaskirche/eterna-philips sessions

bach	**schreier**	lp: philips 422 0881
johannes-	leipzig radio	cd: philips 422 0882/454 1082
passion	chorus	*excerpts*
	alexander	lp: eterna 728 033
	ihle	
	lipovsek	
	schreier	
	bär	
	holl	
	junghanns	
	scheibner	
	wagner	

orchestral soloists: wolfram just, peter seydel and siegfried pank, violas; joachim bischof, cello; werner zeibig, double bass; johannes walter, flute; andreas lorenz, bernhard mühlbach and manfred krause, oboes; wolfgang liebscher and bernhard rose, bassoons; christine schornsheim, organ; raphael alpermann, harpsichord; monika rost, lute

301/30 april-3 may 1988/lukaskirche/eterna-emi sessions

mozart	**vonk**	lp: eterna 728 023
la finta	bär	cd: emi CDC 749 5652
giardiniera		
excerpt		
(der verliebte		
italiener);		
le nozze di		
figaro excerpts		
(se vuol ballare;		
non piu andrai;		
aprite un po		
quel' occhi!;		
hai gia vinta		
la causa);		
don giovanni		
excerpts		
(deh vieni alla		
finestra; finch'		
han dal vino);		
cosi fan tutte		
excerpt		
(donne mie la fata);		
zaide excerpt		
(nur mutig mein herze)		

mozart	lp: eterna 728 023
concert arias:	cd: emi CDC 749 5652
mentre ti lascio;	
un bacio di mano	

mozart	**vonk**	lp: eterna 728 023
zauberflöte	bär	cd: emi CDC 749 5652
excerpts	selbig	
(der vogelfänger	thümmler	
bin ich ja!;	merkel	
ein mädchen	kolditz	
oder weibchen;		
papagena! papageno!)		

sonnhild fiebach, harpsichord soloist

302/26-27 may 1988/kulturpalast/radio ddr

wagner	**vonk**	unpublished radio broadcast
rienzi overture;	prague radio	
strauss	chorus	
die frau ohne		
schatten		
symphonic		
fantasy;		
verdi		
4 pezzi sacri		

303/9-11 september 1988/lukaskirche/eterna-emi sessions

beethoven	**vonk**	cd: emi CDC 754 0762/CMS 763 9372/
piano concerto	zacharias	CDE 574 5572
no 3		

304/18-23 september 1988/lukaskirche/eterna-philips sessions

mozart	**davis**	cd: philips 426 2362
symphony		
no 34		
mozart		lp: philips 416 1551
symphonies		cd: philips 416 1552
nos 35		
"haffner"		
and 38		
"prague"		
mozart		lp: philips 422 2361
symphonies		cd: philips 422 2362
nos 36		
"linz"		
and 40		

305/5-9 november 1988/lukaskirche/eterna-philips sessions

weber	**varviso**	lp: eterna 729 251/826 251
der freischütz	leipzig radio	lp: philips 422 4101
excerpt	chorus	cd: philips 422 4102

(was gleicht
wohl auf erden);
nicolai
die lustigen
weiber von windsor
excerpt
(o süsser mond);
mozart
die zauberflöte
excerpt
(o isis und osiris);
wagner
der fliegende
holländer
excerpt
(steuermann
lass die wacht!);
lohengrin excerpts
(treulich geführt;
gesegnet soll sie
schreiten);
meistersinger
von nürnberg
excerpts
(wach auf!; ehrt eure
deutschen meister!)

305/concluded beethoven fidelio excerpt (o welche lust!)	**varviso** leipzig radio chorus wagner schiller	lp: eterna 729 251/826 251 lp: philips 422 4101 cd: philips 422 4102
wagner der fliegende holländer excerpt (summ und brumm!)	**varviso** leipzig radio chorus peckova	lp: eterna 729 251/826 251 lp: philips 422 4101 cd: philips 422 4102
wagner parsifal excerpt (wein und brot des letzten mahles)	**varviso** leipzig radio chorus dresdner kapellknaben kastner	lp: eterna 729 251/826 251 lp: philips 422 4101 cd: philips 422 4102

Staatskapelle Dresden

2. und 3. Februar 1989
20 Uhr, Kulturpalast

8. Sinfoniekonzert

*Zum 75. Todestag Ernst von Schuchs
am 10. Mai 1989
und
zum 125. Geburtstag von Richard Strauss
am 11. Juni 1989*

Dirigent
Herbert Blomstedt

RICHARD STRAUSS
(1864–1949)

Till Eulenspiegels lustige Streiche
Nach alter Schelmenweise
– in Rondeauform –
für großes Orchester gesetzt, op. 28

Metamorphosen
Studien für 23 Solostreicher

Pause

Tod und Verklärung
Tondichtung für großes Orchester,
op. 24

306/january 1989/lukaskirche/eterna-philips sessions
recordings in these sessions were completed in july and september 1989
mozart **schreier** cd: philips 426 2742
cosi fan tutte schreier
excerpt
(un aura amorosa);
entführung
aus dem serail
excerpts
(o wie ängstlich;
wenn der freude;
ich baue ganz);
la clemenza
di tito excerpt
(se all' impero);
zauberflöte
excerpt
(dies bildnis);
don giovanni
excerpts
(dalla sua pace;
il mio tesoro);
idomeneo excerpts
(non temer amato
bene; fuor del mar)
peter mirring, violin soloist in non temer amato bene

307/5-9 february 1989/lukaskirche/eterna-denon sessions
strauss **blomstedt** cd: denon CO 73801
till eulenspiegels
lustige streiche;
tod und
verklärung;
metamorphosen

308/26-27 april 1989/lukaskirche/eterna sessions
zimmermann **zimmermann** cd: berlin classics BC 91082/BC 93942
nouveaux damm
divertissements
for horn and
orchestra

309/28-29 august 1989/lukaskirche/eterna-emi sessions
beethoven   **vonk**   cd: emi CDC 754 0762/CMS 763 9372
piano concerto   zacharias
no 1

310/16-20 september 1989/lukaskirche/eterna-emi sessions
haydn   **marriner**   cd: emi CDC 754 0022/CZS 568 5922
mass no 7   leipzig radio
"kleine   chorus
orgelmesse"   hendricks

haydn   **marriner**   cd: emi CDC 754 0022/CMS 565 8392
mass no 13   leipzig radio
"schöpfungs- chorus
messe"   hendricks
              murray
              blochwitz
              hölle

311/october 1989/lukaskirche/eterna sessions
final independent eterna recording sessions before german reunification
handel   **vonk**   cd: berlin classics BC 31762
radamisto   ude
excerpt
(höchste wonne
ihr zu dienen)
sonnhild fiebach, harpsichord soloist

mozart   cd: berlin classics BC 31762
zauberflöte
excerpt
(dies bildnis);
entführung
aus dem serail
excerpt
(o wie ängstlich);
nicolai
lustige weiber
von windsor
excerpt
(horche die lerche
singt im hain);
donizetti
l'elisir d'amore
excerpt
(una furtiva lagrima);
tchaikovsky
evgeny onegin
(faint echo of my youth);
auber fra diavolo
excerpt
(ja diese freunde);
strauss
der rosenkavalier
excerpt
(di rigor armato)

311/concluded
donizetti   **vonk**   cd: berlin classics BC 31762
don pasquale   selbig
excerpt   ude
(tornami a dir)

bizet   **vonk**   cd: berlin classics BC 31762
les pecheurs   ude
de perles   scheibner
excerpt
(au fond du
temple saint)

312/november 1989/lukaskirche/eterna-philips sessions
beethoven   **haitink**   cd: philips 426 3082
fidelio   dresden opera   *excerpts*
                  chorus   cd: philips 438 4962
                  norman   cd: dg 459 3902
                  coburn   *performance includes leonore no 3 overture*
                  goldberg   *as a separate track*
                  blochwitz
                  moll
                  wlaschiha
                  schmidt

313/15-24 january 1990/lukaskirche/philips sessions
weber   **davis**   cd: philips 426 3192
der freischütz   leipzig radio   *excerpts*
                  chorus   cd: philips 438 4972
                  mattila
                  lind
                  araiza
                  wlaschiha
                  scheibner
                  s.lorenz
                  moll

orchestral soloists: friedemann jähnig, viola; jan vogler, cello

314/13 march 1990/siegen siegerlandhalle/westdeutscher rundfunk
weber	**blomstedt**	cd: calig CAL 50110-50111
oberon overture;		*concert in the birthplace of fritz busch on his*
reger		*centenary; reger and brahms works were conducted*
variations on a		*by busch at his first dresden concert; concert was*
theme of mozart;		*also performed in dresden on 9 and 10 march 1990*
brahms		
symphony no 2		

315/21 april 1990/lukaskirche/dg sessions
bruckner   **sinopoli**   cd: dg 431 6842
symphony
no 3

316/june 1990/lukaskirche/emi sessions
mozart   **vonk**   cd: emi CDC 754 1382/CDM 566 9872/
clarinet   meyer   CDM 566 9492
concerto

mozart   **vonk**   cd: emi CDC 754 1382/CDM 566 9872/
sinfonia   meyer   CDM 566 9492
concertante   jonas
for wind   schneider
                 azzolini

317/21-30 august 1990/lukaskirche/emi sessions
strauss   **haitink**   cd: emi CDS 754 2592
rosenkavalier   dresden opera   *excerpts*
                 chorus   cd: emi CDC 754 4932
                 kanawa
                 hendricks
                 otter
                 leech
                 rydl
                 grundheber

318/november 1990/lukaskirche/philips sessions
strauss   **ozawa**   cd: philips 432 1532
salome   norman   *excerpts*
               witt   cd: dg 459 3902
               raffeiner
               leech
               morris

319/november-december 1990/lukaskirche/dg sessions
dvorak   **levine**   cd: dg 447 7542
symphony
no 8

320/17-21 january 1991/lukaskirche/philips sessions
bach   **schreier**   cd: philips 432 9722/454 1082
mass in   leipzig radio
b minor   chorus
               auger
               murray
               lipovsek
               schreier
               scharinger

orchestral soloists: peter mirring, violin; peter bruns, cello; reiner barchmann, double bass; ekhart haupt, flute; andreas lorenz and manfred krause, oboes; erik reike and thomas berndt, bassoons; peter lohse, trumpet; erich markwart, horn; raphael alpermann, organ

PHILIPS

HUMPERDINCK
HÄNSEL UND GRETEL

Ann Murray
Edita Gruberova
Christa Ludwig
Gwyneth Jones

Franz Grundheber
Barbara Bonney
Christiane Oelze

Staatskapelle Dresden

SIR COLIN DAVIS

321/24 february-3 march 1991/lukaskirche/philips sessions
mozart **davis** cd: philips 432 9772
symphonies
nos 30;
no 31 "paris";
no 32 and
no 33

beethoven cd: philips 434 1202/446 0672
symphony
no 3
"eroica";
egmont overture

322/september 1991/lukaskirche/dg sessions
strauss **sinopoli** cd: dg 435 7902
ein heldenleben
kai vogler, violin soloist

strauss cd: dg 435 7902
don juan

bruckner cd: dg 435 7862
symphony
no 7

323/13-18 january 1992/lukaskirche/philips sessions
beethoven **davis** cd: philips 446 0672
symphony
no 6
"pastoral"

humperdinck **davis** cd: philips 438 0132
hänsel und dresden opera *excerpts*
gretel chorus cd: philips 442 4352
 gruberova
 murray
 bonney
 jones
 ludwig
 oelze
 grundheber

324/may-june 1992/lukaskirche/dg sessions
schubert   **sinopoli**   cd: dg 437 6892
symphony
no 8
"unfinished";
symphony
no 9
"great"

325/5-18 september 1992/lukaskirche/philips sessions
beethoven   **davis**   cd: philips 446 0672
symphony
no 2;
symphony
no 5;
symphony
no 7

326/december 1992-january 1993/lukaskirche/dg sessions
schumann   **sinopoli**   cd: dg 439 9232
symphony
no 3
"rhenish";
symphony
no 4

327/10-11 january 1993/semperoper/mitteldeutscher rundfunk
webern   **sinopoli**   unpublished radio broadcast
five pieces;   ishai
beethoven   vogler
triple concerto;   bruns
mendelssohn
symphony no 4
"italian"

328/4-5 april 1993/semperoper/dg live recording
strauss   **sinopoli**   cd: dg 439 8992
eine   *concert also included weber oberon overture and*
alpensinfonie   *wagner wesendonk-lieder (soloist m.price)*

329/30 may-1 june 1993/semperoper/dg live recording
schumann **sinopoli** cd: dg 439 9232/459 3902
symphony *concert also included webern six pieces op 6 and*
no 1 *strauss 4 letzte lieder (soloist studer)*
"spring"

330/2-5 june 1993/lukaskirche/dg sessions
strauss **sinopoli** cd: dg 439 8652
4 letzte lieder; studer
wagner
wesendonk-
lieder;
tristan und
isolde prelude
and liebestod

331/7-9 july 1993/lukaskirche/philips sessions
beethoven **davis** cd: philips 446 0672
symphony dresden opera
no 9 chorus
"choral" sweet
rappé
frey
grundheber

332/august 1993/lukaskirche/dg session
schumann **sinopoli** cd: dg 445 8752
overture *recording completed in october 1993*
scherzo and
finale

333/6-17 september 1993/lukaskirche/philips sessions
beethoven **davis** cd: philips 446 0672
symphony
no 1;
symphony
no 4;
symphony
no 8;
leonore no 3
overture

334/17-18 october 1993/semperoper/dg live recording
schumann **sinopoli** dg: cd 439 9232
symphony
no 2

335/15-18 february 1994/lukaskirche/rca-bmg sessions
schubert **davis** cd: rca/bmg 09026 626732
symphony
no 3;
symphony
no 5;
symphony
no 6

335a/19 february 1994/semperoper/mitteldeutscher rundfunk
berlioz **davis** cd: private issue vienna
grande messe dresden opera
des morts chorus
  sinfoniechor
  dresden
  ikaia-purdy

336/27-28 march 1994/semperoper/dg live recording
schumann **sinopoli** cd: dg 445 8752
das paradies dresden opera
und die peri chorus
  faulkner
  grant murphey
  quivar
  wilke
  lewis
  swensen
  hale

337/12 april 1994/semperoper/live recording
nono **sinopoli** unpublished private recordimg
incontri; bruns
haydn
cello concerto
in c;
brahms
symphony
no 2

338/november-december 1994/lukaskirche/dg sessions
dvorak   **levine**   cd: dg 447 7542
symphony
no 9
"new world"

339/december 1994/lukaskirche/dg sessions
bruckner   **sinopoli**   cd: dg 445 7442
symphony
no 8

strauss   cd: dg 445 7442/459 3902
metamorphosen

340/9-10 april 1995/semperoper/dg live recording
liszt   **sinopoli**   cd: dg 449 1372
a faust   dresden opera   *concert also included wagner götterdämmerung*
symphony   chorus   *immolation scene (soloist hass)*
                   cole

341/may 1995/lukaskirche/dg sessions
weber   **sinopoli**   cd: dg 449 2162
der freischütz;
oberon overtures

strauss   cd: dg 449 2162
feuersnot
love scene;
salome
dance of the
7 veils;
die frau ohne
schatten
symphonic
fantasy

wagner   cd: dg 449 1652
rienzi overture;   *tannhäuser overture only also on dg 459 3902*
das liebesverbot
overture;
tannhäuser overture
and bacchanale;
parsifal prelude
and karfreitagszauber

342/may 1995/lukaskirche/dg sessions

sibelius violin concerto; serenades for violin and orchestra nos 1 and 2; humoresque for violin and orchestra   **previn** mutter   cd: dg 447 8952

343/27-29 august 1995/semperoper/teldec live recording

schoenberg gurrelieder   **sinopoli** dresden opera chorus leipzig radio chorus prague mens' chorus voigt larmore moser riegel weikl brandauer   cd: teldec 4509 984242 *also unpublished video recording*

344/2-9 october 1995/lukaskirche/rca-bmg sessions

schubert symphony no 1; symphony no 2; symphony no 4 "tragic"   **davis**   cd: rca/bmg 09026 626732

345/15-17 october 1995/semperoper/teldec live recording
berg	**sinopoli**	cd: teldec 0630 181552
violin	watanabe	*concert also included busoni berceuse élégaique*
concerto		*and tchaikovsky symphony no 6 "pathétique"*

346/january 1996/lukaskirche/dg sessions
mahler	**sinopoli**	cd: dg 453 4372/471 4512
das lied von	vermillion	
der erde	lewis	

347/11-13 january 1996/semperoper/mitteldeutscher rundfunk
haydn	**sinopoli**	unpublished radio broadcast
cello concerto	h.chang	
in c;	vermillion	
mahler	lewis	
das lied von		
der erde		

348/march 1996/lukaskirche/teldec sessions
beethoven	**haitink**	cd: teldec 0630 131592/3984 268012
piano concerti	schiff	
nos 1 and 2		
beethoven		cd: teldec 0630 131592/3984 268022
piano concerto		
no 4		

349/31 march-1 april 1996/semperoper/dg live recording
beethoven	**sinopoli**	cd: dg 453 4232
symphony	dresden opera	
no 9	chorus	
"choral"	kringelborn	
	palmer	
	moser	
	titus	

350/26-28 may 1996/semperoper/teldec live recording
schoenberg	**sinopoli**	cd: teldec 3984 229012
erwartung	marc	

351/2-4 july 1996/lukaskirche/rca-bmg sessions
schubert   **davis**   cd: rca/bmg 09026 626732/09026 685472
symphonies
no 8
"unfinished"
and no 9
"great"

352/5-9 september 1996/lukaskirche/rca-bmg sessions
mozart   **davis**   cd: rca/bmg 09026 686612
idomeneo   kasarova
excerpts
(non ho colpa;
ah quel gelido
orror; il padre
adorato);
lucio silla excerpt
(il tenero momento);
le nozze di figaro
excerpt
(non so piu);
don giovanni
excerpts
(vedrai carino;
mi tradi);
cosi fan tutte
excerpt
(smanie implacabili!);
la clemenza di tito
excerps
(ecco il punto; non
piu di fiori vaghe;
deh per questo);
mitridate excerpt
(venga pur minacci);
io ti lascio o cara,
concert aria

mozart   **davis**   cd: rca/bmg 09026 686612
marches from
idomeneo and
la clemenza di tito

353/15 september 1996/semperoper/zdf television
concert for the 1996 german phono-akademie awards

wagner	**sinopoli**	unpublished video recording
meistersinger	mae	*concert also included solo performances without*
von nürnberg	maisky	*orchestra by sophie mautner, john williams and*
overture;	meyer	*ludwig güttler brass ensemble*
lohengrin	caballé	
act 3 prelude;	seiffert	
wagner		
die walküre		
excerpt		
(winterstürme);		
strauss		
dance of the		
7 veils/salome;		
puccini		
gianni schicchi		
excerpt (o mio		
babbino caro);		
mozart		
clarinet concerto		
second movement;		
tchaikovsky		
two movements from		
rococo variations;		
bruch		
allegro from		
scottish fantasy		

354/september-october 1996/lukaskirche/teldec sessions
webern   **sinopoli**   cd: teldec 3984 229022
im sommerwind;
passacaglia;
six pieces op 6;
five pieces op 10;
symphony;
concerto for
9 instruments;
variations for
orchestra

355/november 1996/lukaskirche/teldec sessions
beethoven   **haitink**   cd: teldec 0630 131592/3984 268022
piano concerto   schiff
nos 3

beethoven   cd: teldec 0630 131592/3984 268002
piano concerto
no 5
"emperor"

356/november 1996/lukaskirche/teldec session
berg   **sinopoli**   cd: teldec 0630 181552
chamber   lucchesini
concerto   watanabe

357/20 november-4 december 1996/semperoper/teldec live recording
strauss   **sinopoli**   cd: teldec 0630 131562
die frau ohne   dresden opera   *also unpublished video recording*
schatten   chorus
                    voigt
                    hass
                    schwarz
                    heppner
                    grundheber
orchestral soloists: roland straumer, violin; jan vogler, cello

SÄCHSISCHE STAATSOPER DRESDEN SEMPEROPER

Mittwoch, den 4. Dezember 1996, 18.00 Uhr

DIE FRAU OHNE SCHATTEN

Oper in drei Aufzügen
von Hugo von Hofmannsthal

Musik von
RICHARD STRAUSS

Mit freundlicher Unterstützung durch die Dresdner Bank

Musikalische Leitung	Giuseppe Sinopoli
Inszenierung	Hans Hollmann
Bühnenbild und Kostüme	rosalie
Choreinstudierung	Matthias Brauer

6. Vorstellung seit der Premiere am 17. November 1996

Dresdner Bank
Förderer der Sächsischen Staatskapelle Dresden

358/december 1996/lukaskirche/teldec sessions
wagner   **runnicles**   cd: teldec 0630 171092
das rheingold
entry of the gods;
die walküre
walkürenritt and
wotans abschied
and feuerzauber;
siegfried
waldweben and
siegfried idyll;
götterdämmerung
rhine journey and
funeral march

359/january 1997/lukaskirche/rca-bmg sessions
berlioz   **davis**   cd: rca/bmg 09026 687902
overtures
le roi lear;
les francs juges;
beatrice et bénedict;
waverley;
le carnaval romain;
benvenuto cellini;
le corsair;
les troyens a carthage

360/23-24 march 1997/semperoper/dg live recording
bruckner   **sinopoli**   cd: dg 457 5872
symphony   *concert also included stravinsky symphony of psalms*
no 9

361/8-11 june 1997/semperoper/teldec live recording
berg	**sinopoli**	cd: teldec 3984 229042
three pieces	banse	*banse replaced bonney as soloist; concert also*
op 6;		*included beethoven symphony no 7*
7 frühe lieder		

362/june 1997/lukaskirche/teldec sessions
schoenberg	**sinopoli**	cd: teldec 3984 229012
pierrot	castellani	
lunaire	lucchesini	
	kai vogler	
	jan vogler	
	haupt	
	becker	
	weise	
	schindler	

363/12-14 july 1997/semperoper/teldec live recording
berg	**sinopoli**	cd: teldec 3984 229042
altenberg-	marc	*concert also included strauss also sprach zarathustra*
lieder		

364/7-9 september 1997/semperoper/teldec live recording
schoenberg	**sinopoli**	cd: teldec 3984 229052
6 orchester-	marc	*concert also included schubert symphony no 4*
lieder		*"tragic" and scriabin poeme de l'extase*

365/september 1997/lukaskirche/emi sessions
haydn	**sinopoli**	cd: emi CDC 556 5352
cello concerti	h.chang	
in c and d;		
lo speziale overture		

365a/october 1997/semperoper/mdr television
mozart	**davis**	unpublished video recording
le nozze di	dresden opera	
figaro	chorus	
	margiono	
	selbig	
	james	
	dorn	
	bär	

366/9-11 november 1997/semperoper/teldec live recording
berg   **sinopoli**   cd: teldec 3984 229032
three pieces   voigt   *concert also included schumann violin concerto*
from the   *(soloist k.vogler) and brahms academic festival*
lyric suite;   *overture*
der wein

367/january 1998/lukaskirche/rca-bmg sessions
mozart   **davis**   cd: rca/bmg 74321 566982/74321 825212
overtures:
cosi fan tutte;
il re pastore;
die zauberflöte;
schauspieldirektor;
le nozze di figaro;
idomeneo;
bastien et bastienne;
don giovanni;
die entführung
aus dem serail;
la clemenza di tito;
la finta giardiniera;
lucio silla

368/april 1998/lukaskirche/teldec session
schoenberg   **sinopoli**   cd: teldec 3984 229052
chamber
symphony

369/5-6 april 1998/semperoper/dg live recording
liszt   **sinopoli**   cd: dg 457 6142
dante   dresden opera   *concert also included schumann genoveva overture*
symphony;   chorus
busoni
sarabande
und cortege

370/20-22 april 1998/berlin adlershof vttv studio/hessisches fernsehen
wagner   **sinopoli**   unpublished video recording
parsifal prelude;   *soundtrack recording for the hessisches fernsehen-*
beethoven   *arte television film "traumpfade der musik"*
symphony no 7;
schumann
symphony no 3
"rhenish"

371/23-24 april 1998/berlin adlershof vttv studio/hessisches fernsehen
strauss   **sinopoli**   unpublished video recording
metamorphosen;   *soundtrack recording for the hessisches fernsehen*
schoenberg   *film by giuseppe sinopoli "die beiden augen des*
verklärte nacht   *horus": a journey through ancient egypt directed*
                                             by barrie gavin

372/31 may-2 june 1998/semperoper/teldec live recording
schoenberg   **sinopoli**   cd: teldec 3984 229052
ein überlebender   dresden opera   *concert also included brahms symphony no 2 and*
aus warschau   chorus   *wagner wotan's farewell and magic fire music from*
                        tomlinson   *die walküre*

373/june 1998/semperoper/teldec session
schoenberg   **sinopoli**   cd: teldec 3984 229052
begleitmusik
zu einer
lichtspielszene

374/15-16 june 1998/semperoper/teldec live recording
berg   **sinopoli**   cd: teldec 3984 229032
symphonic   marc   *concert also included strauss salome closing scene*
fragments   *and beethoven symphony no 3*
from wozzeck

375/22 september 1998/semperoper/mdr television
vivaldi   **sinopoli**   dvd: arthaus musik 100 028
concerto per   *concert for the orchestra's 450th anniversary*
l'orchestra   *celebration with works which were given their first*
di dresda;   *performances in dresden; concert also included rihm*
weber   *vers une symphonie fleuve IV*
jubel overture;
wagner
rienzi overture;
strauss
eine alpensinfonie

376/3 october 1998/theaterplatz/zdf television
open-air klassik-gala for the orchestra's 450th anniversary

weber oberon overture; wagner walkürenritt/ die walküre; verdi la forza del destino overture	**sinopoli**	unpublished video recording

puccini la boheme excerpt (donde lieta usci)	**sinopoli** marc

verdi il trovatore excerpt (ah si ben mio); luisa miller excerpt (quando le sere)	**sinopoli** la scola

wagner die walküre excerpt (winterstürme)	**sinopoli** seiffert

377/january 1999/lukaskirche/rca-bmg sessions

haydn symphony no 104 "london"; berlioz symphonie funebre et triomphale	**davis** dresden opera chorus	rca/bmg unpublished *recordings incomplete*

378/28-29 march 1999/semperoper/dg live recording
bruckner **sinopoli** cd: dg 469 5272
symphony
no 5

379/11 july 1999/theaterplatz/mdr television
open-air klassik-gala
bizet **sinopoli** dvd: emi DVA 492 5009
carmen prelude
and danse boheme;
verdi
la traviata prelude;
nabucco overture;
luisa miller
overture;
aida ballet music

puccini **sinopoli** dvd: emi DVA 492 5009
madama gheorghiu
butterfly alagna
excerpt
(vogliatemi bene);
verdi
otello excerpt
(gia nella notte)

puccini **sinopoli** dvd: emi DVA 492 5009
madama gheorghiu
butterfly
excerpt
(un bel di);
verdi
la forza del
destino excerpt
(pace pace!)

bizet **sinopoli** dvd: emi DVA 492 5009
carmen excerpt alagna
(la fleur que tu
m'avais jetée);
puccini
tosca excerpt
(e lucevan
le stelle)

379/concluded
bizet **sinopoli** dvd: emi DVA 492 5009
carmen excerpt dresden opera
(les voici!); chorus
verdi
il trovatore
excerpt
(vedi le fosche!);
nabucco excerpt
(va pensiero!);
aida excerpts
(gloria all'egitto;
vieni o guerriero
vindice)

380/7 september 1999/semperoper/mdr television
strauss **davis** dvd: arthaus 100 170
ariadne anthony
auf naxos martinez
koch
villars
adam
junge

381/8-9 september 1999/semperoper/dg live recording
strauss **sinopoli** cd: dg 463 4932
josephslegende *concert also included strauss horn concerto no 1*
complete *(soloist markwart)*
scenario

382/september 1999/lukaskirche/dg sessions
strauss **sinopoli** cd: dg 463 4942
friedenstag dresden opera
chorus
voigt
botha
villars
dohmen

383/16-17 april 2000/semperoper/dg live recording
dvorak   **sinopoli**   cd: dg 471 0332
stabat mater   dresden opera
chorus
zvetkova
donose
botha
scandiuzzi

384/3 september 2000/theaterplatz/arte-zdf television
open-air opera concert

weber   **sinopoli**   unpublished video recording
oberon overture;   *ballet music not recorded in dresden was added to*
wagner   *the television transmission*
walkürenritt/
die walküre;
verdi
la forza del
destino overture;
puccini
manon lescaut
intermezzo

wagner   **sinopoli**
entry of the   dresden opera
guests/   chorus
tannhäuser;
puccini
turandot excerpt
(perche tarda
e la luna);
verdi nabucco
excerpt
(va pensiero)

384/concluded
verdi   **sinopoli**   unpublished video recording
il trovatore   martinez
excerpt
(tacea la notte);
puccini la boheme
excerpt
(si mi chiamano mimi);
puccini
madama butterfly
excerpt
(un bel di)

puccini   **sinopoli**
tosca excerpt   armiliato
(recondita
armonia);
la boheme excerpt
(che gelida manina);
la fanciulla
del west excerpt
(che' ella mi creda)

puccini   **sinopoli**
la boheme   martinez
excerpt   armiliato
(o soave fanciulla)

verdi   **sinopoli**
la forza del   nucci
destino excerpt
(urna fatal);
macbeth excerpt
(pieta rispetto
amore)

puccini   **sinopoli**
tosca excerpt   dresden opera
(tre sbirri!)   chorus
                 nucci

385/september 2000/lukaskirche/dg sessions
strauss	**sinopoli**	cd: dg 471 3232
ariadne auf	voigt	*excerpts*
naxos	dessay	cd: dg 471 4722
	von otter	
	heppner	
	dohmen	

386/3 december 2000/frauenkirche/mdr television
bach	**sinopoli**	unpublished video recording
weihnachts-	dresden opera	*concert to matk the first stage of the completion*
oratorium	chorus	*of rebuilt frauenkirche*
excerpt	bartoli	

(jauchzet frohlocket!);
mozart
exsultate jubilate;
vivaldi
concerto per dresda;
mozart
vesperae solennes
excerpt
(laudate dominum);
vivaldi
concerto in a;
bach
mass in b minor
excerpts
(laudamus te;
dona nobis pacem)

387/9-11 january 2001/semperoper/mitteldeutscher rundfunk
strauss	**sinopoli**	cd: private issue vienna
tod und		
verklärung;		
ein heldenleben		

strauss	**sinopoli**	unpublished radio broadcast
horn concerto	damm	
no 2		

388/13-14 february 2001/semperoper/live recording
verdi	**sinopoli**	cd: frauenkirche dresden
messa da	dresden opera	*sinopoli's last recording, produced by bkl srudios*
requiem	chorus	*in aid of the frauenkirche re-building fund*
	sinfoniechor	
	dresden	
	dessi	
	fiorillo	
	botha	
	scandiuzzi	

389/8 june 2001/lukaskirche/erato sessions
beethoven	**davis**	cd: erato awaiting publication
ah perfido!;	mattila	
fidelio excerpt (abscheulicher!);		
weber euryanthe excerpt (so bin ich nun verlassen);		
der freischütz excerpts (und ob die wolke; leise leise);		
oberon excerpt (ozean du ungeheuer!);		
mendelssohn infelice, concert aria		

390/june 2001/lukaskirche/koch sessions
beethoven	**davis**	cd: koch awaiting publication
piano concerto no 3	gourari	

CITTA' DI FIRENZE
TEATRO COMUNALE
Ente Autonomo

AMICI DELLA MUSICA

DOMENICA 24 NOVEMBRE 1957 - ORE 17,15

CONCERTO SINFONICO

DRESDNER STAATSKAPELLE

PROGRAMMA

MOZART - Sinfonia n. 40 in sol min (K. 550)
        Allegro molto
        Andante
        Minuetto (Allegretto)
        Allegro assai

STRAUSS - Morte e trasfigurazione - poema sinfonico

BEETHOVEN - Sinfonia n. 3 in mi bem magg., op. 55 («Eroica»)
        Allegro con brio
        Marcia funebre (Adagio assai)
        Scherzo (Allegro vivace)
        Finale (Allegro molto)

Direttore
LOVRO von MATACIC

PREZZI

Palchi (escluso ingresso)	L. 6.000	Prima gradinata numerata	L. 600
Ingresso ai palchi	» 500	Seconda gradinata numerata	» 400
Poltrone	» 2.000	Loggione numerato	» 250

Informazioni, prenotazione e vendita dei biglietti:
BIGLIETTERIA DEL TEATRO COMUNALE
Corso Italia 16, tel. 26.253

MOVIMENTO FORESTIERI   UNIVERSALTURISMO
Via Vecchietti 22, tel. 26.361   Via Speziali 7 r., tel. 294.541

In caso di necessità l'Ente Autonomo del Teatro Comunale si riserva il diritto di modificare il presente programma.

appendix a: recordings falsely attributed to sächsische staatskapelle dresden

During the 1950s a series of budget lps was produced by the record Corporation of America of Union City NJ, mainly on the Allegro label, which were taken from tapes acquired from both East and West Germany but which were published with pseudonymous names of orchestras and conductors. One of the names commonly used for these unofficial publications was that of an ensemble referred to as "Dresden State Symphony Orchestra under the conductor Fritz Schreiber".

Thanks to the assiduous research of Ernst Lumpe it is possible to identify the correct provenance of at least some of the LPs attributed to Dresden forces, and these are listed here :-

allegro 1487: rachmaninov piano concerto 3/soloist harry reims
this is actually decca recording LXT 2701 with moura lympany and the new symphony orchestra conducted by anthony collins

allegro royale 1412: wagner lohengrin preludes and two scenes
performers unidentified

allegro royale 1430: weber der freischütz excerpts
this is actually drawn from the complete decca recording LXT 2597-2599 with the vienna philharmonic orchestra conducted by otto ackermann

allegro toyale 1431: mozart cosi fan tutte excerpts in german
performers unidentified

allegro royale 1462: stravinsky oiseau de feu and kabalevsky the comedians (these performances attributed to "dresden symphony orchestra conducted by max von berten")
stravinsky unidentified; kabalevsky possibly taken from discovery DL 4003 with paris philharmonic conducted by methen

allegro royale 1468: ravel daphnis et chloe second suite & ma mere l'oye
performers unidentified

allegro royale 1518-1519: humperdinck hänsel und gretel
this is actually deutsche grammophon recording LPEM 19007-19008 with munich philharmonic orchestra conducted by fritz lehmann

allegro elite 3086: wagner das rheingold scenes (also issued on gramophone 20139)
these excerpta are actually taken from a 1952 broadcast by ndr hamburg with ndr orchestra conducted by wilhelm schüchter

allegro elite 3090: mozart die entführung aus dem serail excerpts
these excerpts are actually taken from a 1946 broadcast by ndr hamburg with ndr orchestra conducted by hans schmidt-isserstedt

allegro elite 3095: wagner parsifal prelude and act 3 extract
these excerpts are actually taken from a 1951 or 1952 bayreuth broadcast with bayreuth festival orchestra conducted by hans knappertsbusch; they are not taken from the 1951 version officially published by decca/telefunken

allegro elite 3098: tchaikovsky evgeny onegin scenes in german
tatiana's letter scene is the dg recording LPEM 19023 with elfriede trötschel and the munich philharmonic orchestra conducted by robert heger; the balance (including another version of the letter scene with annelies kupper) is taken from a 1950 munich broadcast with bavarian radio orchestra conducted by hans altmann; an additional version of the opera's prelude remains unidentified

allegro elite 3111: beethoven symphonies 1 and 8
performers unidentified

allegro elite 3113: beethoven symphony 3 "eroica" (also issued in uk by pickwick as allegro ALL 701)
this performance gained a certain notoriety for having been attributed to a version conducted by wilhelm furtwängler: this remains unproven, and other names put forward include erich kleiber, eugen jochum and herbert von karajan; subsequent issues on cd, still with the attribution "dresden state symphony orchestra conducted by fritz schreiber", seem to contain an entirely different performance to the one on the original allegro lp

allegro elite 3114: beethoven symphony 5
performers unidentified

allegro elite 3115: beethoven symphony 6 "pastoral"
performers unidentified

allegro elite 3117-3118: beethoven symphony 9 "choral"
this unidentified performance states the usual attribution "dresden state symphony orchestra and dresden state opera chorus conducted by fritz schreiber" on the front cover and record labels but "berlin symphony orchestra and berlin cathedral choir conducted by gerd rubahn" on the back cover; it also states on front cover of the lps that beethoven's namensfeier overture is included, but this is not the case. to the writer this version bears remarkable similarities to one conducted in leipzig in 1951 by hermann abendroth

allegro elite 3122: brahms symphony 2
performers unidentified

allegro elite 3123: brahms symphony 3
Performers unidentified

allegro elite 3124: brahms symphony 4 (also issued as allegro royale 1239 with a different attribution "berlin symphony orchestra conducted by franz t. friedl")
performers unidentified

allegro elite 4010: stravinsky les noces
this is a 1953 cologne broadcast with the wdr orchestra conducted by jean martinon

additional publication containing the attribution "dresden symphony orchestra conducted by ernest weir"
aries LP 1631: havergal brian symphony 2
this is actually a 1973 bbc recording with kensington symphony orchestra conducted by leslie head

according to klaus heinze there may have been an allegro lp of scenes from wagner's götterdämmerung (with the standard attribution of "dresden state symphony orchestra conducted by fritz schreiber") but actually drawn from a 1950s bayreuth festival performance

appendix b: index of conductors

asterisk against conductor's name indicates that he held position of generalmusikdirektor or that of a chief conductor; numbers referred to are session numbers and not page numbers

amabile

MOZART

SYMPHONIEN
Symphonies
NR. 36 „LINZER" · *"Linz"*
NR. 38 „PRAGER" · *"Prague"*

HIGH PERFORMANCE CLASSICS · HIGH PERFORMANCE Q

DEUTSCHE SCHALLPLATTEN

Staatskapelle Dresden
KAREL ANČERL

claudio abbado/born 1933

158

hermann abendroth/1883-1956

070a

karel ancerl/1908-1973

080

gerhard rolf bauer/born 1932

139

paavo berglund/born 1929

216

gary bertini/born 1927

191

herbert blomstedt, generalmusikdirektor 1975-1985

herbert blomstedt/born 1927

167	173	177	179
182	186	195	196
200	206	208	208a
209	210	215	217
220	222	227	228
230	231	233	236
238	239	242	243
245	247	249	251
253	256	259	268
270	271	278	283
292	294	307	314

"HIS MASTER'S VOICE"
RECORD LIBRARY SERIES
No. 329

DIE MEISTERSINGER
VON NÜRNBERG
(WAGNER)

THIRD ACT

ORIGINAL GERMAN TEXT
with the
ENGLISH SINGING VERSION

By arrangement with
SCHOTT & CO., LTD.,
Owners of the Copyright
(All rights reserved)

Price
Two Shillings and Sixpence

GREATEST ARTISTS  FINEST RECORDING

The Hallmark of Quality

THE GRAMOPHONE COMPANY, LTD., HAYES, MIDDLESEX

*karl böhm/1894-1981

007	008	008a	010
011	012	013	014
014a	015	016	017
018	019	020	021
022	023	024	025
026	028	029	031
032	074	076	078
086	126	160	172
211	224	225	

heinz bongartz/1894-1978

124

willi boskovsky/1909-1991

207

karl elmendorff, generalmusikdirektor 1943-1945

*fritz busch/1890-1951

003	004	005	006

colin davis/born 1927

252	266	272	297
304	313	321	323
325	331	333	335
335a	344	351	352
359	365a	367	377
380	389	390	

*karl elmendorff/1891-1962

033	033a	034	034a
037	038	039	040
041	042	043	044
045	046		

Sunday 4th March 2001 at 7.30pm **Royal Festival Hall**

DRESDEN
STAATSKAPELLE OF SAXONY
Bernard Haitink conductor

IN THE PRESENCE OF **HRH** THE DUKE OF KENT,
ROYAL PATRON OF THE DRESDEN TRUST

MOZART
Symphony No.38 in D major, Prague

interval

BRUCKNER
Symphony No. 3 in D minor (1877 version)

Programme: £2.00

Part of:

CLASSIC INTERNATIONAL

DRESDNER BANK AG – Sponsors of the Dresden Staatskapelle

carl von garaguly/1900-1984

149

peter gülke

227

*bernard haitink/born 1929

312   317   348   355

nikolaus harnoncourt/born 1929

267

wolf dieter hauschild/born 1937

275

robert heger/1886-1978

108

hans werner henze/born 1926

114

heinrich hollreiser/born 1913

181

eugen jochum during a bruckner recording session

marek janowski/born 1941

180	198	219	221
237	244	250	254
262			

eugen jochum/1902-1987

119	193	199	201
204	214	218	223
229a	234	235	

herbert von karajan/1908-1989

140	159	197a

herbert kegel/1920-1990

129	130	141	144

*joseph keilberth/1908-1968

050	051	052

*rudolf kempe/1910-1976

054	055	056	057
058	060	061	063
071a	121a	123	136
137	146	154	164
165	169	176	190
194			

bernhard klee/born 1936

212

carlos kleiber/born 1930

166   241

hans knappertsbusch/1888-1965

072   082   083

kyrill kondrashin/1914-1981

70   099a

*franz konwitschny/1902-1962

064   065   066   067
068   069   071   075
79   081

gustav kuhn/born 1947

277

232
*siegfried kurz/born 1930

089	113	120	121
147	178	184	188
192	197	202	203
213	246	257	260
263	264		

james levine/born 1943

291   319   338

hans löwlein/born 1909

053   059   062

leopold ludwig/1908-1979

073

neville marriner/born 1924

258 279 287 310

rudolf mauersberger/1889-1971

077

francesco molinari-pradelli/1911-1996

145

franz peter müller-sybel

134 185

vittorio negri/born 1923

135 156 163 170

*rudolf neuhaus/1914-1990

111

seiji ozawa/born 1935

318

234
giuseppe patané/1932-1989

109   147   162

andré previn/born 1929

342

kurt redel/born 1918

110

ernst richter/born 1903

053

heinz rögner/born 1929

132   141   171

hans joachim rotzsch/born 1929

185

donald runnicles/born 1954

358

*kurt sanderling/born 1912

087	095	106	116
148	151	153	157

wolfgang sawallisch/born 1923

112   143   161

hans schmidt-isserstedt/1900-1973

142

paul schmitz/1899-1992

102

peter schreier/born 1935

205	255	269	289
299	300	306	320

helmut seydelmann/1901-1962

092

kresimir siepuch/born 1930

150

giuseppe sinopoli at a rehearsal in january 2001 with peter damm, principal horn

*giuseppe sinopoli/1946-2001

295	315	322	324
326	327	328	329
330	332	334	336
337	339	340	341
343	345	346	347
349	350	353	354
356	357	360	361
362	363	364	365
366	368	369	370
371	372	373	374
375	376	378	379
381	382	383	384
385	386	387	388

horst stein/born 1928

084

richard strauss/1864-1949

009

*kurt striegler/1886-1958

019a	030	035	036
047	048		

STAATSKAPELLE DRESDEN
Träger des Vaterländischen Verdienstordens

Freitag, den 14. September 1962, 20 Uhr,
im Großen Haus der Staatstheater

1. SINFONIEKONZERT

Dirigent: OTMAR SUITNER

Joseph Haydn
(1732–1809)

Sinfonie Nr. 100, G-Dur

Adagio – Allegro
Allegretto
Menuetto: Moderato
Finale: Presto

Claude Debussy
(1862–1918)

Prélude à l'après-midi d'un faune

(Vorspiel zum Nachmittag eines Fauns)

PAUSE

Igor Strawinski
(geb. 1882)

Le sacre du printemps

(Das Frühlingsopfer)

(Neufassung 1947)

*otmar suitner/born 1922

085	088	090	091
093	094	096	097
098	099	100	101
103	103a	104	105
115	117	118	122
125	127	128	131
133	138	152	155
168	175	183	187
232			

george szell/1897-1970

107

jeffrey tate/born 1943

284   293

silvio varviso/born 1924

189   265   305

240
hans vonk/born 1942

248	273	276	277
282	285	288	296
298	301	302	303
309	311	316	

edo de waart/born 1941

163   174

konrad wagner/born 1930

226   240   261

hiroshi wakasugi/born 1935

274   280   286

heinz wallberg/born 1923

229

hans hendrik wehding/born 1915

049

udo zimmermann/born 1943

308

david zinman/born 1936

281

appendix c: index of works

the designation "excerpts" includes both orchestral (overtures) and vocal sections; numbers referred to are session numbers and not page numbers

242

adolphe adam/si j'étais roi – overture

285

eugen d'albert/tiefland – excerpts

102

daniel-francois auber/fra diavolo

043

fra diavolo – excerpts

285 311

johann sebastian bach/concerti for 2, 3 and 4 harpsichords bwv 1061-1065

110

johannes-passion

300

mass in b minor

077 320

mass in b minor – excerpts

386

matthäus-passion

269

weihnachtsoratorium

289

weihnachtsoratorium – excerpt

386

bela bartok/piano concerto no 3

159

ludwig van beethoven/symphony no 1

233   333

symphony no 2

233   325

symphony no 3 "eroica"

066   173   195   280
321

symphony no 4

220   333

244
symphony no 5

208   325

symphony no 6 "pastoral"

209   321

symphony no 7

137   186   284   325
370

symphony no 8

215   231   333

symphony no 9 "choral"

025   228   278   331
349

piano concerto no 1

290   309   348

piano concerto no 2

288   297   348

piano concerto no 3

017   197a   290   303
355   390

piano concerto no 4

015	208a	272	288
348			

piano concerto no 5 "emperor"

018	208a	272	298
355			

violin concerto

19	273

triple concerto

327

egmont – overture

007	069	137	321

fidelio

051	126	312

fidelio – excerpts

033a	042	048	069
305	389		

leonore

196

246
leonore no 3 – overture

14   338

die weihe des hauses – overture

284

grosse fuge

041

ah perfido – concert aria

389

alban berg/violin concerto

345

chamber concerto

356

three pieces

361

three pieces from the lyric suite

366

wozzeck – symphonic fragments

374

altenberg-lieder

363

sieben frühe lieder

361

der wein – concert aria

366

theodor berger/rondino giocoso

022

hector berlioz/grande messe des morts

335a

symphonie funebre et triomphale

377

benvenuto cellini – overture

359

248
béatrice et bénédict – overture

359

carnaval romain – overture

359

le corsair – overture

359

la damnation de faust – marche hongroise

022

les francs juges – overture

359

le roi lear – overture

359

les troyens a carthage – prelude

359

waverley – overture

359

georges bizet/symphony in c

155

carmen

032

carmen – excerpts

003	053	062	113
162	265	379	

les pecheurs de perles – excerpts

152   311

francois boieldieu/harp concerto in c

246

la dame blanche – excerpt

113

alexander borodin/symphony no 2

087

in the steppes of central asia

087

250
johannes brahms/symphony no 1

148

symphony no 2

005   082   151   314
337

symphony no 3

072   157   158

symphony no 4

017   044   153   229a

piano concerto no 1

075

piano concerto no 2

017   229a

violin concerto

023   065

academic festival overture

171

tragic overture

153

haydn variations

071a 157 158

hungarian dances

171

hungarian dances – excerpts

014

benjamin britten/sinfonia da requiem

194

variations and fugue on a theme of purcell

141

max bruch/allegro from the scottish fantasy

353

252
anton bruckner/symphony no 1

223

symphony no 2

234

symphony no 3

107   204   315

symphony no 4 "romantic"

008   193   251   295

symphony no 5

011   235   378

symphony no 6

218

symphony no 7

201   239   322

symphony no 8

121a   199   339

symphony no 9

214   360

ferruccio busoni/sarabande und cortege for the opera doktor faust

369

max butting/piano concerto

132

emanuel chabrier/espana

258

peter cornelius/der barbier von bagdad – excerpts

033a   285

claude debussy/prélude a l'apres-midi d'un faune

097

carl ditters von dittersdorf/harp concerto in a flat

171

254
gaetono donizetti/don pasquale – excerpts

054   147   311

l'elisir d'amore – excerpt

311

la favorita – excerpt

033a

nico dostal/manina – excerpts

033a

antonin dvorak/symphony no 8

179   319

symphony no 9 "from the new world"

071a   338

slavonic rhapsody no 3

216

scherzo capriccioso

216

the jacobin – excerpt

033

rusalka

052

stabat mater

383

gottfried von einem/konzert für orchester

045

prinzessin turandot – excerpt from the ballet

034a

edward elgar/cello concerto

258

introduction and allegro for strings

258

cockaigne – overture

258

256

hanns eisler/ernste gesänge

103

gabriel fauré/requiem

272

johann peter fick/horn concerto in e flat

213

fidelio finke/capriccio on a polish song for piano and orchestra

132

friedrich von flotow/alessandro stradella – overture

285

martha – excerpts

023a   033a   285

jean francaix/le roi nu – ballet suite

030

jeux poétiques pour harpe et orchestre

171

césar franck/symphony in d minor

106

alberto ginastera/harp concerto

246

umberto giordano/andrea chenier – excerpt

048

mikhail glinka/caprice brillant

258

christoph willibald gluck/orfeo ed euridice – dance of the blessed spirits

003

hermann goetz/der widerspenstigen zähmung

034

charles gounod/faust – excerpts

016   067   152

258

edvard grieg/peer gynt – incidental music

210

george frideric handel/harp concerto in b flat

171

ariodante – excerpt

113

radamisto – excerpt

311

johann adolf hasse/te deum

240

regina coeli

226

gloria from mass in d minor

226

franz josef haydn/symphony no 45 "farewell"

095

symphony no 88

083

symphony no 92 "oxford"

084

symphony no 93

119

symphony no 94 "surprise"

119

symphony no 95

119

symphony no 98

119

symphony no 103 "drum roll"

084

260
symphony no 104 "london"

95   377

cello concerto in c

337   347   365

cello concerto in d

365

feldpartita für bläser

089

lo speziale – overture

365

mass no 7 "kleine orgelmesse"

310

mass no 9 "heiligmesse"

287

mass no 10 "in tempore belli"

279

mass no 11 "nelsonmesse"

279

mass no 12 "theresienmesse"

287

mass no 13 "schöpfungsmesse"

310

die jahreszeiten – excerpt

033a

hans werner henze/musen siziliens

114

paul hindemith/symphonic metamorphoses on themes of weber

071a   117

wolfgang hohensee/hier bin ich mensch – film symphony in 5 movements

129

262
engelbert humperdinck/hänsel und gretel

128   323

hänsel und gretel – excerpt

016

igelhoff/eine nacht mit rosita – excerpt

033a

leos janacek/kata kabanova – excerpt

053

siegfried köhler/symphony no 3

197

piano concerto

203

karel komzak/bad'ner madln – waltz

229

wilfried krätzschmar/cataracta per orchestra

296

rainer kunad/quadrophonie für 4 streichorchester, blechbläser und pauken

178

siegfried kurz/piano concerto

120

horn concerto

184

concerto for trumpet and strings

188

paul kurzbach/concertino for piano and strings

121

josef lanner/hofballtänze – waltz

131

264
schönbrunner – waltz

131

stryrische tänze – waltz

131

jean-marie leclair/oboe concerto in c

156

franz lehar/gold und silber – waltz

164

giuditta – excerpt

033a

der graf von luxemburg – excerpt

033a

ruggiero leoncavallo/i pagliacci – excerpts

013 014a 033a 048
109

franz liszt/dante symphony

369

faust symphony

340

carl loewe/hochzeitslied and heinrich der vogler

047

albert lortzing/undine – excerpts

007   113   152

der wildschütz – excerpt

035

zar und zimmermann

108

zar und zimmermann – excerpts

007   113   285

konzertstück for horn and orchestra

264

266
gustav mahler/symphony no 1

97   286

symphony no 4

073

das lied von der erde

346   347

alessandro marcello/oboe concerto in d minor

156

heinrich marschner/hans heiling – excerpt

027

frank martin/ballade for flute and strings

263

pietro mascagni/cavalleria rusticana – excerpts

013   021   265

jules massenet/manon – excerpt

113

méditation from thais

265

siegfried matthus/piano concerto

182

responso

231

felix mendelssohn-bartholdy/symphony no 3 "scotch"

063

symphony no 4 "italian"

327

violin concerto

219

infelice – concert aria

389

a midsummer night's dream – scherzo

003

268
ernst-hermann meyer/des sieges gewissheit for tenor, chorus and orchestra

185

giacomo meyerbeer/l'africaine – excerpt

054

wolfgang amadeus mozart/symphony no 28

175   252

symphony no 29

85   252

symphony no 30

175   321

symphony no 31 "paris"

122   321

symphony no 32

175   321

symphony no 33

091   321

symphony no 34

175   304

symphony no 35 "haffner"

122   304

symphony no 36 "linz"

080   122   304

symphony no 38 "prague"

080   122   173   259
304

symphony no 39

183   252   259

symphony no 39 – menuetto

003

symphony no 40

187   249   304

symphony no 41 "jupiter"

069   168   249   252

270
piano concerto no 15

090

piano concerto no 21

100

piano concerto no 22

281

piano concerto no 23

281

piano concerto no 26

070a

bassoon concerto

260

clarinet concerto

260   316

clarinet concerto – second movement

353

sinfonia concertante for wind

93 316

flute concerto no 1

167

flute concerto no 2

167

andante in c for flute and orchestra

167

horn concerto no 1

177

horn concerto no 2

177

horn concerto no 3

24 177

horn concerto no 4

177

272
rondo for horn and orchestra k371

177

flute and harp concerto

187

oboe concerto

167

violin concerto no 3

014   064

divertimenti k136-138

200

serenade no 2

168

serenade no 4

174

serenade no 5

174

serenade no 6 "serenata notturna"

070a   088

serenade no 7 "haffner"

174   267

serenade no 9 "posthorn"

163   267

serenade no 13 "eine kleine nachtmusik"

014   088

adagio and fugue in c minor

206

maurerische trauermusik

299

ein musikalischer spass

091

notturno for 4 orchestras

168

274

march in d k215

174

march in d k237

174

march in d k249

174 267

two marches in d k335

163 267

ave verum corpus

299

coronation mass

299

exsultate jubilate

212 386

laudate dominum k321

212

mass in c minor

299

requiem

255

vesperae solennes de confessore

299

vesperae solennes de confessore – excerpt

212   386

dir seele des weltalls – cantata

299

laut verkünde unsre freude – cantata

299

die maurerfreude – cantata

299

ascanio in alba – excerpt

282

276
bastien et bastienne – excerpt

367

la clemenza di tito

225

la clemenza di tito – excerpts

118	282	305	352
367			

cosi fan tutte

033a	054	115	118
282	301	306	352
367			

don giovanni

040

don giovanni – excerpts

038	057	115	118
128	282	301	306
352	367		

die entführung aus dem serail

094	172

die entführung aus dem serail – excerpts

017	038	118	152
282	306	311	367

la finta giardiniera – excerpts

282	301	367

idomeneo

142	211

idomeneo – excerpts

282	306	352	367

lucio silla – excerpts

282	352	367

mitridate – excerpt

352

le nozze di figaro

105	365a

le nozze di figaro – excerpts

003	017	033	035
115	128	282	301
352	367		

il re pastore – overture

367

278
der schauspieldirektor

172

der schauspieldirektor – excerpt

282

zaide – excerpts

128   301

die zauberflöte

138   266

die zauberflöte – excerpts

003	054	115	118
128	152	282	301
305	306	311	367

a berenice sol nascente – concert aria

133   253

a questo seno deh vieni – concert aria

227

ah lo previdi – concert aria

222

ah non sai qual pensa – concert aria

133

ah se in ciel benigne stelle – concert aria

227

alcandro lo confesso – concert aria

253

un bacio di mano – concert aria

301

bella mia fiamma – concert aria

256

betracht dies herz – concert aria

212

chi sa chi sa qual sia – concert aria

227

clarice cara mia sposa – concert aria

242

280

con ossequio con rispetto – concert aria

242

ein ergrimmter löwe brüllt – concert aria

212

fra cento affanni – concert aria

133   253

hat der schöpfer dieses lebens – concert aria

212

io ti lascio o cara – concert aria

352

ma che vi fece o stelle – concert aria

133   227

männer suchen stets zu naschen – concert aria

128

mentre ti lascio o figlio – concert aria

301

mia speranza adorata – concert aria

133   222

misera dove son – concert aria

256

misero o sogno – concert aria

242

misero pargoletto – concert aria

227

no che non sei capace – concert aria

091   133   227

non curo l'affetto – concert aria

133   253

non so d'onde viene – concert aria

253

non temer amato bene – concert aria

091

per pieta non ricercate – concert aria

242

282
per questa bella mano – concert aria

096

popoli di tessaglia – concert aria

222

quel nocchier che in gran procella – concert aria

212

schon lacht der holde frühling – concert aria

222

se al labbro mio non oredi – concert aria

242

simostro la sorte – concert aria

242

sperai vivino il lido – concert aria

133

tali e colanti – concert aria

242

va dal furor – concert aria

242

voi avete un cor fedele – concert aria

133   227

vorrei spiegarvi o dio – concert aria

91   253

modest mussorgsky/boris godunov – excerpts

054   067   130

otto nicolai/die lustigen weiber von windsor – excerpts

113   285   305   311

luigi nono/incontri

337

siegfried ochs/variations on 's kommt ein vogel geflogen

229

jacques offenbach/les contes d'hoffmann – excerpts

265   293

284
carl orff/die kluge – excerpts

036

hans pfitzner/symphony in c op 46

025 031

amilcare ponchielli/la gioconda – excerpts

023a 265

serge prokofiev/symphony no 1 "classical"

070

peter and the wolf

144

giacomo puccini/la boheme – excerpts

376 384

la fanciulla del west – excerpts

024 384

gianni schicchi – excerpt

353

madama butterfly – excerpts

059   379   384

manon lescaut – excerpts

265   384

tosca – excerpts

048   379   384

turandot – excerpts

004   048   162   384

maurice ravel/boléro

258

max reger/violin concerto

247

variations on a theme of mozart

010   124   314

joseph reicha/concerto for 2 horns and orchestra

213

286
emil von reznicek/donna diana – overture

013   285

nikolai rimsky-korsakov/mozart und salieri

237

gerhard rosenfeld/piano concerto

139

violin concerto no 2

192

cello concerto

139

giaochino rossini/il barbiere di siviglia – excerpts

036   067

la gazza ladra – overture

265

l'italiana in algeri

191

camille saint-saens/morceau de concert for horn and orchestra

264

samson et dalila – bacchanale

265

ludwig schmidseder/die heimkehr nach mittenwald – excerpt

023a

arnold schoenberg/begleitmusik zu einer lichtspielszene

373

erwartung

350

gurrelieder

343

kammersinfonie

368

6 orchesterlieder

364

288

pierrot lunaire

362

ein überlebender aus warschau

372

verklärte nacht

371

franz schmidt/notre dame – intermezzo

265

franz peter schubert/symphony no 1

112   247   344

symphony no 2

112   243   344

symphony no 3

112   217   335

symphony no 4 "tragic"

041   112   238   344

symphony no 5

| 029 | 112 | 205 | 236 |
| 335 | | | |

symphony no 6

| 112 | 230 | 335 |

symphony no 8 "unfinished"

| 112 | 205 | 217 | 324 |
| 351 | | | |

symphony no 9 "great"

| 056 | 112 | 224 | 245 |
| 284 | 324 | 351 | |

three symphonic fragments arranged by gülke

227

overtures in c and d in the italian style

112

rosamunde – incidental music

207

marche militaire

022

290
mass no 5 d678

143

mass no 6 d950

143

robert schumann/symphony no 1 "spring"

161   329

symphony no 2

161   334

symphony no 3 "rhenish"

161   326   370

symphony no 4

072   159   161   326

piano concerto

026

violin concerto

219

konzertstück for 4 horns and orchestra

264

manfred – overture

161

overture, scherzo and finale

161 332

das paradies und die peri

336

dimitri shostakovich/symphony no 4

099a

symphony no 10

197a

symphony no 11 "year 1905"

079

292

jean sibelius/violin concerto

342

two serenades for violin and orchestra

342

humoresque for violin and orchestra

342

bedrich smetana/ma vlast

216

the bartered bride – excerpts

003   022   152

johann matthias sperger/horn concerto in e flat

213

johann strauss/ägyptischer marsch

149

an der schönen blauen donau – waltz

232

annen polka

232

auf der jagd – polka

149

czardas from ritter pasman

229

elyen a magyar – polka

232

die fledermaus – overture

003   016   164

freikugeln – polka

232

g'schichten aus dem wienerwald – waltz

164

kaiserwalzer

022   149

im krapfenwaldl – polka

149

294
künstlerleben – waltz

232

leichtes blut – polka

164

morgenblätter – waltz

149

eine nacht in venedig – overture

229

neue pizzicato polka

229

perpetuum mobile

149

rosen aus dem süden – waltz

149

1001 nacht – intermezzo

013

tritsch-tratsch polka

149

unter donner und blitz – polka

232

vergnügungszug – polka

232

wiener blut – waltz

149

wo die zitronen blüh'n – waltz

229

johann strauss father/radetzky marsch

232

josef strauss/auf ferienreisen – polka

131

dorfschwalben aus österreich – waltz

232

296
feuerfest – polka

131

frauenherz polka

131

die libelle – polka

131

mein lebenslauf ist lieb' und lust – waltz

232

moulinet polka

131

plappermäulchen – polka

131

sphärenklänge – waltz

164

richard strauss/eine alpensinfonie

| 076 | 146 | 328 | 375 |

also sprach zarathustra

| 103a | 146 | 292 |

aus italien

176

der bürger als edelmann

136

der bürger als edelmann – excerpt

003

couperin suite

169

don juan

| 016 | 076 | 136 | 294 |
| 322 | | | |

don quixote

| 009 | 169 |

298
ein heldenleben

074　　　　146　　　　271　　　　322
387

josephslegende

381

josephslegende – symphonic fragment

176

macbeth

165

metamorphosen

068　　　　103a　　　　104　　　　165
307　　　　339　　　　371

schlagobers waltz

146

sinfonia domestica

071　　　　154

till eulenspiegels lustige streiche

009　　　　025　　　　076　　　　081
136　　　　307

tod und verklärung

083   136   160   307
387

burleske for piano and orchestra

190

duett-concertino for clarinet and bassoon

190

horn concerto no 1

103a   132   190

horn concerto no 2

132   190   387

oboe concerto

190

panathenäenzug for piano and orchestra

190

parergon zur sinfonia domestica

190

violin concerto

190

300
wind serenade op 7

089

vier letzte lieder

231   330

arabella – excerpts

28   111

ariadne auf naxos

123   380   385

capriccio – excerpts

113   125   136

daphne – excerpts

016   125

elektra

086

feuersnot – love scene

341

die frau ohne schatten

357

die frau ohne schatten – excerpts

| 028 | 125 | 302 | 341 |

friedenstag

382

intermezzo – act two entr'acte

136

der rosenkavalier

| 058 | 078 | 257 | 276 |
| 317 | | | |

der rosenkavalier – excerpts

001	002	008a	013
025	054	111	125
169	311		

salome

| 050 | 101 | 318 |

302
salome

050   101   318

salome – excerpts

016   035   136   341
353

die schweigsame frau

198

die schweigsame frau – excerpt

125

igor stravinsky/l'oiseau de feu – ballet suite

194

le sacre du printemps

099

franz von suppé/flotte burschen – overture

127

jolly robbers – overture

127

light cavalry – overture

127

morning noon and night in vienna – overture

127 164

poet and peasant – overture

127

die schöne galathea – overture

03 127

piotr tchaikovsky/symphony no 5

213

violin concerto

064 150 248

rococo variations for cello and orchestra – excerpt

353

serenade for strings

099

304

capriccio italien

16   258

casse noisette

277

casse noisette – excerpt

003

evgeny onegin

291

evgeny onegin – excerpts

055   113   277   311

romeo and juliet – fantasy overture

087

georg philipp telemann/concerto in g for oboe d'amore and orchestra

156

der schulmeister – cantata

096

giuseppe verdi/messa da requiem

388

messa da requiem – excerpt

033a

quattro pezzi sacri

302

aida – excerpts

022 162 265 379

attila – excerpt

189

un ballo in maschera – excerpt

189

don carlo – excerpt

189 265

falstaff – excerpt

189

306
la forza del destino – excerpts

004	035	055	109
152	189	376	379
384			

i lombardi – excerpt

265

luisa miller – excerpts

037	376

macbeth – excerpt

265	384

nabucco – excerpts

265	379	384

otello – excerpts

023a	024	030	033a
092	189	265	379

rigoletto

145

rigoletto – excerpts

147	189

la traviata – excerpts

113   147   379

il trovatore – excerpts

048   189   265   376
384

antonio vivaldi/concerto per dresda

135   375   386

concerto in a

386

concerto in g minor

135

two concerti in c

135

concerto in f for 2 horns and orchestra

213

308
oboe concerto in d minor

156

concerti for viola d'amore and orchestra

163

4 violin concerti in e flat, e minor, a minor and g minor

170

robert volkmann/serenade for strings no 2

118

georg christoph wagenseil/concerto in c for four harpsichords

110

richard wagner/der fliegende holländer – excerpts

| 019a | 020 | 033a | 189 |
| 274 | 305 | | |

götterdämmerung

262

götterdämmerung – excerpts

038   358

das liebesverbot – overture

341

lohengrin – excerpts

016	020	048	054
189	274	305	353

die meistersinger von nürnberg

060   140

die meistersinger von nürnberg – act three

012

die meistersinger von nürnberg – excerpts

003	017	024	030
049	134	189	231
305	353		

parsifal – excerpts

221   305   341   370

das rheingold

244

das rheingold – excerpts

033a   221   358

310
rienzi

181

rienzi – overture

274   302   341   375

siegfried

254

siegfried – excerpts

038   221   358

tannhäuser – excerpts

006   020   021   042
054   189   274   341
384

tristan und isolde

241

tristan und isolde – excerpts

189   330

die walküre

250

die walküre – act one

042

die walküre – excerpts

| 033a | 042 | 221 | 353 |
| 358 | 376 | 384 | |

wesendonk-lieder

330

wesendonk-lieder – excerpts

033

carl maria von weber/symphony no 1

155

piano concerto no 1

270

piano concerto no 2

270

312
konzertstück for piano and orchestra

270

clarinet concerto no 1

116   283

clarinet concerto no 2

116   283

concertino for clarinet and orchestra

283

concertino for horn and orchestra

264

aufforderung zum tanz

003

abu hassan

141

abu hassan – excerpt

277

beherrscher der geister – overture

277

euryanthe

180

euryanthe – excerpts

038　　　　　061　　　　　173　　　　　277
389

der freischütz

039　　　　　061　　　　　165　　　　　275
313

der freischütz – excerpts

014　　　　　016　　　　　027　　　　　277
305　　　　　341　　　　　389

jubel – overture

277　　　　　375

oberon – excerpts

022　　　　　061　　　　　277　　　　　314
341　　　　　376　　　　　384　　　　　389

peter schmoll – excerpt

033a

314
preciosa – overture

277

turandot – overture

277

anton webern/variations for orchestra

354

symphony

354

concerto for nine instruments

354

im sommerwind

354

passacaglia

354

five pieces

327   354

six pieces

354

manfred weiss/symphony no 3

268

concertino for organ, strings and percussion

202

friedrich witt/symphony in c "jena"

071

hugo wolf/der corregidor

046

der könig bei der krönung

047

316
jan dismas zelenka/missa circumcisionis

261

carl ziehrer/hereinspaziert – waltz

229

udo zimmermann/nouveaux divertissements for horn and orchestra

308

miscellaneous/weihnachtslieder

185

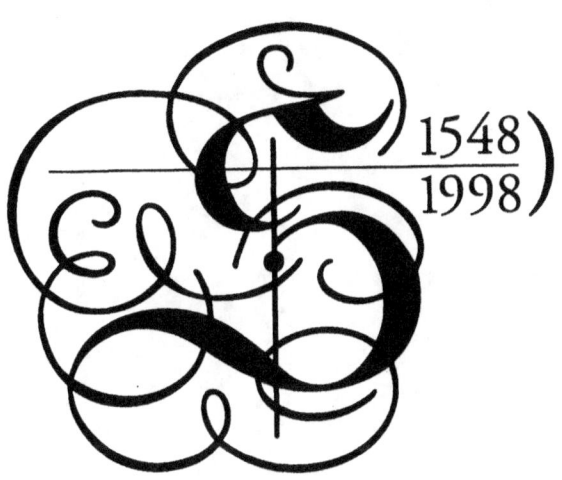

Discographies by Travis & Emery:
Discographies by John Hunt.

1987: 978-1-906857-14-1: From Adam to Webern: the Recordings of von Karajan.
1991: 978-0-951026-83-0: 3 Italian Conductors and 7 Viennese Sopranos: 10 Discographies: Arturo Toscanini, Guido Cantelli, Carlo Maria Giulini, Elisabeth Schwarzkopf, Irmgard Seefried, Elisabeth Gruemmer, Sena Jurinac, Hilde Gueden, Lisa Della Casa, Rita Streich.
1992: 978-0-951026-85-4: Mid-Century Conductors and More Viennese Singers: 10 Discographies: Karl Boehm, Victor De Sabata, Hans Knappertsbusch, Tullio Serafin, Clemens Krauss, Anton Dermota, Leonie Rysanek, Eberhard Waechter, Maria Reining, Erich Kunz.
1993: 978-0-951026-87-8: More 20th Century Conductors: 7 Discographies: Eugen Jochum, Ferenc Fricsay, Carl Schuricht, Felix Weingartner, Josef Krips, Otto Klemperer, Erich Kleiber.
1994: 978-0-951026-88-5: Giants of the Keyboard: 6 Discographies: Wilhelm Kempff, Walter Gieseking, Edwin Fischer, Clara Haskil, Wilhelm Backhaus, Artur Schnabel.
1994: 978-0-951026-89-2: Six Wagnerian Sopranos: 6 Discographies: Frieda Leider, Kirsten Flagstad, Astrid Varnay, Martha Moedl, Birgit Nilsson, Gwyneth Jones.
1995: 978-0-952582-70-0: Musical Knights: 6 Discographies: Henry Wood, Thomas Beecham, Adrian Boult, John Barbirolli, Reginald Goodall, Malcolm Sargent.
1995: 978-0-952582-71-7: A Notable Quartet: 4 Discographies: Gundula Janowitz, Christa Ludwig, Nicolai Gedda, Dietrich Fischer-Dieskau.
1996: 978-0-952582-72-4: The Post-War German Tradition: 5 Discographies: Rudolf Kempe, Joseph Keilberth, Wolfgang Sawallisch, Rafael Kubelik, Andre Cluytens.
1996: 978-0-952582-73-1: Teachers and Pupils: 7 Discographies: Elisabeth Schwarzkopf, Maria Ivoguen, Maria Cebotari, Meta Seinemeyer, Ljuba Welitsch, Rita Streich, Erna Berger.
1996: 978-0-952582-77-9: Tenors in a Lyric Tradition: 3 Discographies: Peter Anders, Walther Ludwig, Fritz Wunderlich.
1997: 978-0-952582-78-6: The Lyric Baritone: 5 Discographies: Hans Reinmar, Gerhard Huesch, Josef Metternich, Hermann Uhde, Eberhard Waechter.
1997: 978-0-952582-79-3: Hungarians in Exile: 3 Discographies: Fritz Reiner, Antal Dorati, George Szell.
1997: 978-1-901395-00-6: The Art of the Diva: 3 Discographies: Claudia Muzio, Maria Callas, Magda Olivero.
1997: 978-1-901395-01-3: Metropolitan Sopranos: 4 Discographies: Rosa Ponselle, Eleanor Steber, Zinka Milanov, Leontyne Price.
1997: 978-1-901395-02-0: Back From The Shadows: 4 Discographies: Willem Mengelberg, Dimitri Mitropoulos, Hermann Abendroth, Eduard Van Beinum.
1997: 978-1-901395-03-7: More Musical Knights: 4 Discographies: Hamilton Harty, Charles Mackerras, Simon Rattle, John Pritchard.
1998: 978-1-901395-94-5: Conductors On The Yellow Label: 8 Discographies: Fritz Lehmann, Ferdinand Leitner, Ferenc Fricsay, Eugen Jochum, Leopold Ludwig, Artur Rother, Franz Konwitschny, Igor Markevitch.
1998: 978-1-901395-95-2: More Giants of the Keyboard: 5 Discographies: Claudio Arrau, Gyorgy Cziffra, Vladimir Horowitz, Dinu Lipatti, Artur Rubinstein.
1998: 978-1-901395-96-9: Mezzo and Contraltos: 5 Discographies: Janet Baker, Margarete Klose, Kathleen Ferrier, Giulietta Simionato, Elisabeth Hoengen.

1999: 978-1-901395-97-6: The Furtwaengler Sound Sixth Edition: Discography and Concert Listing.
1999: 978-1-901395-98-3: The Great Dictators: 3 Discographies: Evgeny Mravinsky, Artur Rodzinski, Sergiu Celibidache.
1999: 978-1-901395-99-0: Sviatoslav Richter: Pianist of the Century: Discography.
2000: 978-1-901395-04-4: Philharmonic Autocrat 1: Discography of: Herbert Von Karajan [Third Edition].
2000: 978-1-901395-05-1: Wiener Philharmoniker 1 - Vienna Philharmonic and Vienna State Opera Orchestras: Discography Part 1 1905-1954.
2000: 978-1-901395-06-8: Wiener Philharmoniker 2 - Vienna Philharmonic and Vienna State Opera Orchestras: Discography Part 2 1954-1989.
2001: 978-1-901395-07-5: Gramophone Stalwarts: 3 Separate Discographies: Bruno Walter, Erich Leinsdorf, Georg Solti.
2001: 978-1-901395-08-2: Singers of the Third Reich: 5 Discographies: Helge Roswaenge, Tiana Lemnitz, Franz Voelker, Maria Mueller, Max Lorenz.
2001: 978-1-901395-09-9: Philharmonic Autocrat 2: Concert Register of Herbert Von Karajan Second Edition.
2002: 978-1-901395-10-5: Sächsische Staatskapelle Dresden: Complete Discography.
2002: 978-1-901395-11-2: Carlo Maria Giulini: Discography and Concert Register.
2002: 978-1-901395-12-9: Pianists For The Connoisseur: 6 Discographies: Arturo Benedetti Michelangeli, Alfred Cortot, Alexis Weissenberg, Clifford Curzon, Solomon, Elly Ney.
2003: 978-1-901395-14-3: Singers on the Yellow Label: 7 Discographies: Maria Stader, Elfriede Troetschel, Annelies Kupper, Wolfgang Windgassen, Ernst Haefliger, Josef Greindl, Kim Borg.
2003: 978-1-901395-15-0: A Gallic Trio: 3 Discographies: Charles Muench, Paul Paray, Pierre Monteux.
2004: 978-1-901395-16-7: Antal Dorati 1906-1988: Discography and Concert Register.
2004: 978-1-901395-17-4: Columbia 33CX Label Discography.
2004: 978-1-901395-18-1: Great Violinists: 3 Discographies: David Oistrakh, Wolfgang Schneiderhan, Arthur Grumiaux.
2006: 978-1-901395-19-8: Leopold Stokowski: Second Edition of the Discography.
2006: 978-1-901395-20-4: Wagner Im Festspielhaus: Discography of the Bayreuth Festival.
2006: 978-1-901395-21-1: Her Master's Voice: Concert Register and Discography of Dame Elisabeth Schwarzkopf [Third Edition].
2007: 978-1-901395-22-8: Hans Knappertsbusch: Kna: Concert Register and Discography of Hans Knappertsbusch, 1888-1965. Second Edition.
2008: 978-1-901395-23-5: Philips Minigroove: Second Extended Version of the European Discography.
2009: 978-1-901395--24-2: American Classics: The Discographies of Leonard Bernstein and Eugene Ormandy.

Discography by Stephen J. Pettitt, edited by John Hunt:
1987: 978-1-906857-16-5: Philharmonia Orchestra: Complete Discography 1945-1987

Available from: Travis & Emery at 17 Cecil Court, London, UK. (+44) 20 7 240 2129. email on sales@travis-and-emery.com .

© Travis & Emery 2009

Music and Books published by Travis & Emery Music Bookshop:
Anon.: Hymnarium Sarisburiense, cum Rubricis et Notis Musicis.
Agricola, Johann Friedrich from Tosi: Anleitung zur Singkunst.
Bach, C.P.E.: edited W. Emery: Nekrolog or Obituary Notice of J.S. Bach.
Bateson, Naomi Judith: Alcock of Salisbury
Bathe, William: A Briefe Introduction to the Skill of Song
Bax, Arnold: Symphony #5, Arranged for Piano Four Hands by Walter Emery
Burney, Charles: The Present State of Music in France and Italy
Burney, Charles: The Present State of Music in Germany, The Netherlands ...
Burney, Charles: An Account of the Musical Performances ... Handel
Burney, Karl: Nachricht von Georg Friedrich Handel's Lebensumstanden.
Cobbett, W.W.: Cobbett's Cyclopedic Survey of Chamber Music. (2 vols.)
Corrette, Michel: Le Maitre de Clavecin
Crimp, Bryan: Dear Mr. Rosenthal ... Dear Mr. Gaisberg ...
Crimp, Bryan: Solo: The Biography of Solomon
d'Indy, Vincent: Beethoven: Biographie Critique
d'Indy, Vincent: Beethoven: A Critical Biography
d'Indy, Vincent: César Franck (in French)
Frescobaldi, Girolamo: D'Arie Musicali per Cantarsi. Primo & Secondo Libro.
Geminiani, Francesco: The Art of Playing the Violin.
Handel; Purcell; Boyce; Geene et al: Calliope or English Harmony: Volume First.
Häuser: Musikalisches Lexikon. 2 vols in one.
Hawkins, John: A General History of the Science and Practice of Music (5 vols.)
Herbert-Caesari, Edgar: The Science and Sensations of Vocal Tone
Herbert-Caesari, Edgar: Vocal Truth
Hopkins and Rimboult: The Organ. Its History and Construction.
Hunt, John: Adam to Webern: the recordings of von Karajan
Isaacs, Lewis: Hänsel and Gretel. A Guide to Humperdinck's Opera.
Isaacs, Lewis: Königskinder (Royal Children) A Guide to Humperdinck's Opera.
Kastner: Manuel Général de Musique Militaire
Lacassagne, M. l'Abbé Joseph : Traité Général des élémens du Chant.
Lascelles (née Catley), Anne: The Life of Miss Anne Catley.
Mainwaring, John: Memoirs of the Life of the Late George Frederic Handel
Malcolm, Alexander: A Treaty of Music: Speculative, Practical and Historical
Marx, Adolph Bernhard: Die Kunst des Gesanges, Theoretisch-Practisch
May, Florence: The Life of Brahms
May, Florence: The Girlhood Of Clara Schumann: Clara Wieck And Her Time.
Mellers, Wilfrid: Angels of the Night: Popular Female Singers of Our Time
Mellers, Wilfrid: Bach and the Dance of God
Mellers, Wilfrid: Beethoven and the Voice of God
Mellers, Wilfrid: Caliban Reborn - Renewal in Twentieth Century Music

Music and Books published by Travis & Emery Music Bookshop:
Mellers, Wilfrid: François Couperin and the French Classical Tradition
Mellers, Wilfrid: Harmonious Meeting
Mellers, Wilfrid: Le Jardin Retrouvé, The Music of Frederic Mompou
Mellers, Wilfrid: Music and Society, England and the European Tradition
Mellers, Wilfrid: Music in a New Found Land: ...... American Music
Mellers, Wilfrid: Romanticism and the Twentieth Century (from 1800)
Mellers, Wilfrid: The Masks of Orpheus: ...... the Story of European Music.
Mellers, Wilfrid: The Sonata Principle (from c. 1750)
Mellers, Wilfrid: Vaughan Williams and the Vision of Albion
Panchianio, Cattuffio: Rutzvanscad Il Giovine
Pearce, Charles: Sims Reeves, Fifty Years of Music in England.
Playford, John: An Introduction to the Skill of Musick.
Purcell, Henry et al: Harmonia Sacra ... The First Book, (1726)
Purcell, Henry et al: Harmonia Sacra ... Book II (1726)
Quantz, Johann: Versuch einer Anweisung die Flöte traversiere zu spielen.
Rameau, Jean-Philippe: Code de Musique Pratique, ou Methodes.
Rastall, Richard: The Notation of Western Music.
Rimbault, Edward: The Pianoforte. Its Origins, Progress, and Construction.
Rousseau, Jean Jacques: Dictionnaire de Musique
Rubinstein, Anton: Guide to the proper use of the Pianoforte Pedals.
Sainsbury, John S.: Dictionary of Musicians. Vol. 1. (1825). 2 vols.
Serré de Rieux, Jean de : Les dons des Enfans de Latone
Simpson, Christopher: A Compendium of Practical Musick in Five Parts
Spohr, Louis: Autobiography
Spohr, Louis: Grand Violin School
Tans'ur, William: A New Musical Grammar; or The Harmonical Spectator
Terry, Charles Sanford: J.S. Bach's Original Hymn-Tunes for Congregational Use.
Terry, Charles Sanford: Four-Part Chorals of J.S. Bach. (German & English)
Terry, Charles Sanford: Joh. Seb. Bach, Cantata Texts, Sacred and Secular.
Terry, Charles Sanford: The Origins of the Family of Bach Musicians.
Tosi, Pierfrancesco: Opinioni de' Cantori Antichi, e Moderni
Van der Straeten, Edmund: History of the Violoncello, The Viol da Gamba ...
Van der Straeten, Edmund: History of the Violin, Its Ancestors... (2 vols.)
Waltern: Musikalisches Lexicon
Walther, J. G.: Musicalisches Lexikon ober Musicalische Bibliothec

Travis & Emery Music Bookshop
17 Cecil Court, London, WC2N 4EZ, United Kingdom.
Tel. (+44) 20 7240 2129

© Travis & Emery 2009

www.ingramcontent.com/pod-product-compliance
Lightning Source LLC
Chambersburg PA
CBHW052052230426
43671CB00011B/1883